Praise for #QUALIFIED

"If you've ever felt unqualified, this book will convince you otherwise. Amanda takes you on a journey to discover what you want, and empowers you to go get it. An inspiring read!"

—*Keith Ferrazzi,* New York Times *#1 Best-Selling Author of* Who's Got Your Back *and* Never Eat Alone

"Amanda wants us to love what we do and make a greater impact in the world. I can already sense the ripple effect of her book."

—*Hal Elrod, Bestselling author of* The Miracle Morning *and* The Miracle Equation

"Step-by-step, Amanda leads you on a journey to your passion career. She empowers you through personal stories and practical, clear advice to make courageous connections that will change your life."

—*Dr. Sarah B. Steinberg, Former Executive Vice Provost, Johns Hopkins University*

"Whether you are a recent college graduate or an experienced executive; Amanda brilliantly connects the dots for everyone who has ever felt unqualified."

—*Jeff M. Jeffries, Director of Employer Relations at Carnegie Mellon University*

"Amanda demystifies the "real world" so you can overcome your doubts and see beyond the societal standards to go after what you want."

—*Laurie Ruettimann, Host of Punk Rock HR*

"Amanda strikes the perfect balance and tone in her discussion of what it takes to achieve your best career and life at any age. Her book encourages readers to give themselves important permission to question and explore their career passions in a way that inspires positive, long-term change and career satisfaction."

—*Alyssa S. Hammond, Director,*
Undergraduate Career Services at Bentley University

"Amanda breaks through intimidating long titles and job descriptions with tangible steps that are within reach."

—*David Stollman, President, Campuspeak*

"Amanda does a stellar job of taking you behind the scenes on how to create a life and career that is truly meaningful!"

—*Scott Anthony Barlow,*
CEO & Founder of Happen to Your Career

"In this book Amanda takes a fresh approach when it comes to creating a career you love. Best of all, you can implement the steps today."

—*John Ruhlin, Author of* Giftology

"Amanda takes you on a journey to discover what you want, and empowers you to go get it."

–Keith Ferrazzi, *New York Times* #1 Best-Selling Author of *Who's Got Your Back* and *Never Eat Alone*

#QUALIFIED

YOU ARE MORE IMPRESSIVE THAN YOU REALIZE

AMANDA NACHMAN
CEO & Publisher of College Magazine

Copyright © 2020 by Amanda Nachman

All rights reserved. No part of this publication may be reproduced, distributed, or transmitted in any form or by any means, including photocopying, recording, digital scanning, or other electronic or mechanical methods, without the prior written permission of the publisher, except in the case of brief quotations embodied in critical reviews and certain other noncommercial uses permitted by copyright law.

When you purchase *#QUALIFIED*, you support Reality Changers, a San Diego nonprofit that helps underserved high school students achieve their dreams of becoming college graduates. We're honored to direct a portion of book sales to Reality Changers.

#QUALIFIED

Edited by Riley Bogh, Rachel Aldrich and Taylor Ulrich
ISBN: 9781950367337

Published by

LifestyleEntrepreneursPress.com

Publications or foreign rights acquisition of our catalog books.
Learn More: *www.LifestyleEntrepreneursPress.com*

Printed in the USA

#QUALIFIED

YOU ARE MORE IMPRESSIVE
THAN YOU REALIZE

AMANDA NACHMAN
CEO & Publisher of College Magazine

WARNING: This book will make you ambitious AF.
Side Effects May Include: Career success. Beyoncé confidence.
A renegade resume. Gold medal mindset.
Loss of apprehension. Read at your own risk.

To my parents, for your love, wisdom, and encouragement.

You showed me that taking action can turn dreams into reality.

CONTENTS

Introduction

WHEN DOUBT SMACKS YOU IN THE FACE

Straight out of college, I felt confident that I had it all figured out. I had found an investor, quit my boring 9-5 job, and turned my hobby business, *College Magazine*, into a career.

But then reality hit, and hit hard.

I was on my third issue of the magazine, and after a full day of distributing thousands of copies at Towson University, I drove into downtown Baltimore to place even more magazines at the nearby restaurants. I hopped out of my car to unload the flimsy plastic dolly and the heavy box of magazines from my trunk. As I went to place my treasured magazines onto the dolly, the box slipped out of my hands and dropped onto the dolly's base—the handle swung up and smacked me directly in the face.

There I stood, bleeding from my mouth, startled and crying in the waning light of a gravel-filled parking lot in downtown Baltimore. My workaholic life flashed before my eyes: 15-hour days spent struggling

1

to get advertisers and running myself ragged distributing magazines by hand—only to wind up broke, exhausted, and now injured.

A wave of doubt rushed in like a tsunami. *Am I really qualified to run my own business?*

Despite my run-in with the dolly, my teeth were still intact, and my bruised lip healed after a week. My determination, though, took longer to recover. I thought about what I had risked by quitting my steady job for the magazine. I had run both my health and my bank account into the ground.

But, I hadn't completely failed (yet), which meant there was still hope of success. *Right?* And if I should fail, I decided I was willing to accept that. *Is failure really so bad?*

At the heart of it all, I still had my "why"—why I fell in love with the experience at *College Magazine*, working with students to create an authentic guide to navigating college.

When I look back, I realize that my rational mind wasn't what kept me going. It was my passion for helping college students through the magazine that fueled me through this difficult time. I had to keep going.

Over the next few months, I finally began hitting my stride.

I won a $15,000 prize in a business competition called Cupid's Cup, sponsored by founder and CEO of Under Armour, Kevin Plank.

A talent manager for RCA Music Group, Jamie Abzug, agreed to a cover story and photoshoot with celebrity musician Mike Posner. Yes, *the* Mike Posner.

I even sold my first year-long advertising campaign to the regional marketing manager at vitaminwater®, Kevin Burke.

Seed money, celebrity cred, and advertising had all materialized in a matter of months. I recommitted to following my passion and believing in myself.

It was up to me and me only to figure out that I was qualified and to keep going.

These victories were defining moments, but they were only just the start to a long journey of successes and failures that would ultimately create my career as it is today— the CEO and publisher of *College Magazine*.

What started as a wee print magazine on one campus in 2007 grew to fourteen campuses on the East Coast by 2012. Today, the publication reaches millions of readers online nationwide at CollegeMagazine.com.

There were days, like the day I threw down with the dolly that made me want to quit.

But I always circled back to my why. My desire for meaningful work. A project that aligned with my interests, strengths, and values.

You are more qualified than you realize and like me, you deserve your passion career too.

What exactly *is* a passion career? It is that perfect storm that brews when your interests, strengths, and values connect to a career you like, and—dare I say—possibly even love.

I've worked with hundreds of college students who have written, edited, and interned at *College Magazine*. I've also worked with dozens of young professionals who have graduated and felt lost about the direction of their career. The underlying, recurring theme that I have witnessed time and time again is that we all struggle to identify a career we love.

But now more than ever, it's vital that you connect your passion to a career. Why? Let me break it down.

- ▶ Our global economy presents a more competitive environment that favors people who are more passionate about their jobs.

- ▶ Passionate people produce better results and make a bigger impact.

► When you love your work, you're eager to build upon your qualifications, helping you dream bigger and achieve more.

What else are you waiting for? Why continue your current job or accept a new one that makes you feel unfilled for 40 *long* hours a week when instead you can do something that inspires you?

There's a ripple effect when you enjoy what you do. You produce quality work that changes lives. Here's a glimpse of what happens when people follow their passions:

► Christian Feliciano changes the lives of the students he coaches through Reality Changers, helping underserved high school students apply to and graduate from college.

► Sarah Bidnick makes theatre more accessible to everyone through her passion career as the senior vice president of marketing at TodayTix.

► Claire Kreger-Boaz creates once-in-a-lifetime moments for music educators and music students through her work at the National Association of Music Merchants (NAMM) and The NAMM Foundation.

► Rachel Aldrich spreads her love for writing and reading working for her dream company, Penguin Random House.

► Carey Smolensky creates memorable and life-changing events for his clients. He also helps the homeless community in Chicago through his company's grassroots initiative, A Warmer Winter, which distributes warm clothing and meals to the homeless community in Chicago every December.

► Andrea Stone, a school counselor, helps her elementary school students work on their emotional intelligence and grow into empathetic human beings, while also helping them solve their day-to-day problems.

▸ Ben Simon reduces food waste as the CEO and co-founder of Imperfect Produce. In fact, he has recovered over 40 million pounds of produce, donated over 2.8 million pounds of food, and created several hundred living-wage jobs.

This is just a few of the people I've spoken to in their passion careers on my *Find Your Passion Career* podcast—and the list goes on.

Don't be fooled, not everyone started in their passion career. Laurence Jackson currently works in his dream job as a Line Producer's Assistant on the Netflix Original *You* and produces SAG short films on the side...but he spent the first four years of his career as an IT auditor for Ernst & Young. Just like Laurence, anyone, including you, can pivot in their career because everything you've learned up to this point is transferable.

You could be doing something you love. Isn't that how you want to spend your time? Do you want to sell something you don't care about or create business plans and presentations for products and services you don't believe in? Of course not. Instead, you should be putting your effort into creating or contributing to your passion career.

Unlike just any old job, in a passion career you will finally feel fulfilled. You'll create value while feeding your soul through your work. And yes, I promise this is all possible.

When I graduated from the University of Maryland, *College Magazine* was only a side hustle. I had networked like crazy my senior year to secure a full-time job working for a government consulting firm. As an unapologetic overachiever, I was incredibly proud of landing a stable job right after graduation at a reputable company that paid well.

I was so dead set on getting the job that I never asked myself if I even wanted it—and unfortunately, I hated it. My day-to-day mainly consisted of red tape research: nothing new, nothing competitive, and nothing creative. Ultimately, I spent nine monotonous months creating slide decks, writing white papers, and attending meetings with government clients all while desperately trying to stay awake by chugging coffee. I felt like I was dying a slow death. I could feel the weight of gravity pulling me past my ergonomic office chair into the depths of the ground, swallowed by the dirt of the Earth. *Too dramatic?* That's honestly what it felt like.

Literally, the only thing I had to look forward to was going home to work on *College Magazine*.

I had launched the magazine earlier that year from my dorm room at the University of Maryland in 2007. I held writer meetings on campus, edited articles, and sold print advertisements to local restaurants.

And I personally hand-distributed thousands of my 32-page, glossy print magazines at Maryland, George Washington, Georgetown, American, Towson, Johns Hopkins, Loyola, and Goucher (because I couldn't afford a professional distribution company at the time).

Eventually, I took action on my plan to ditch my job for *College Magazine*. I sought outside capital, which seemed like the best way to validate my concept and justify quitting my stable job. I met with a couple of business owners and ultimately, I found an investor. After months of negotiating, working with a pro bono lawyer to develop an operating agreement, I quit my job and worked solely on my passion business full time.

I've talked to like-minded high achievers who experienced this same scenario: one day they wake up with a seemingly safe job and say, "Hold up, is this really what I was meant to do?"

Rachel Aldrich, a former editor in chief at *College Magazine*, landed a job after graduating from Boston College as a reporter covering stocks and writing financial articles. After a few months, she found the work mind-numbing and knew she couldn't continue on that path.

The feeling of working on something you don't even care about creeps into other aspects of your life. You start to feel *blah*, unhappy, and simply like you were meant for more but are settling for less.

When I look back on my own experience and I see my students', graduates', and friends' experiences, I realize that many of us are just going through the motions. We're launching our careers without intentionally looking within first. Many of us skip this key first step: We don't take the time to uncover our passion before chasing what we truly want. And even if we realize what we truly want, we often feel discouraged after the first taste of rejection.

You could have the best resume in the world and the highest-paying job, but if you don't love it (or even like it), then you aren't living at your fullest potential. It's certainly not a sustainable model for a fulfilling life. If you're like me, you worked hard in high school and college with the long-term goal of attaining a meaningful career. But how do you make those career aspirations a reality?

Many of my college graduates at *College Magazine* have gone on to achieve their passion careers at inspiring companies like *National Geographic*, Penguin Random House, *USA Today*, *Vox*, *Rachael Ray Every Day* magazine, NBC, *Washingtonian* magazine, and more. Their ambitions were fueled by a passion for journalism.

College Magazine allowed them to glow up. They improved their writing skill sets, confidence, resumes, and interview skills. Our editors led teams of five writers, helping them become stronger journalists. Even with all that, they still experienced doubt—doubt that their writing or leadership skills were strong enough. Doubt about what lies ahead. Doubt that they were properly qualified. Then if they were rejected by the 1-percent opportunities (jobs with enormous brands that you recognize, like Google and Johnson & Johnson) that doubt doubled down.

Rejection is powerful. According to a study by five psychologists, our brains perceive rejection the same as physical pain, which affects

7

our self-esteem. [1] And I've seen it first hand, when you feel unqualified, it holds you back.

The doubt manifests because you haven't realized, embraced, and communicated your passion.

This doubt is a distraction from unlocking, seeking, and achieving your passion career. It's time to stop giving these negative feelings so much power over you. I can't tell you how many people I've spoken to who are in careers they despise but don't even have an answer when I ask them, "How much time have you spent researching careers in industries that interest you?" or "How many people have you talked to in those careers?"

Don't beat yourself up if you haven't even thought about these questions. It took me years to solve the equation for finding a passion career. But once you understand the process, you can make it happen.

Even if you've been working in your career for a decade or longer, it's never too late to hit the pause button. Anyone can follow their passion. Don't think you need to quit your job to get started—take small actions to make your passion career a reality. Now is the time to learn how to speak your passion and connect it to the 99-percent opportunities (in other words, working with lesser-known brands like DuckDuckGo or Public Goods) so that you get can overcome your doubt and find a career you enjoy.

If you wait for someone to confirm that you're qualified, how long would you be waiting? As long as we have waited for Rihanna's new album?

I'm not saying it's always easy. There will definitely be times where you'll feel like you've taken a dolly handle to the face, but it *will* be worth it. Let's start your intentional career journey *now*. Once you uncover your passion, and learn how to take action, you'll start to make courageous connections and ultimately discover how to speak your passion.

When you speak your passion, doors open.

FEEDING YOUR HANGRY SOUL

H ave you ever felt like you're starving for something meaningful, something bigger than yourself? You spend (at least) 40 hours a week working, so shouldn't you be working toward a fulfilling career that doesn't have you counting down the minutes until clock out time? If your appetite is big enough, you can achieve just that.

It's human nature to seek meaningful work. And meaningful work creates a positive impact in the world.

According to the Center for Disease Control, about 40 percent of Americans do not believe their lives have a clear sense of purpose.[2] "Research has shown that having purpose and meaning in life increases overall well-being and life satisfaction, improves mental and physical health, enhances resiliency, enhances self-esteem, and decreases the chances of depression," wrote Emily Esfahani Smith in her article for *The Atlantic*, "There's More to Life Than Being Happy."[3]

When you follow your passion, you connect to experiences that feed your soul. Our souls are hungry, not just for carbs, but for fulfilling projects. It's a feeling that motivates you every morning to show up and give your best. Even those days when your best is fueled by that cold, leftover pizza from the night before.

Why do we need to feed our souls? Because we need something more, beyond money, to keep us engaged. Money can be a motivator, but if you're solely working for a paycheck—pushing paper with no ripple-effect impact, providing no meaning to others, or leaving no legacy—you aren't following a sustainable model for a fulfilling career. When you work a job that feeds your soul, sparks happiness, and makes you feel fulfilled, you've created a sustainable career.

While a job that simply pays the bills can be necessary, it's not ideal. If that's what your life looks like today, that's okay; but tell yourself, *that's for today*.

Meanwhile, ask yourself: *What would life be like if I loved what I did?*

Start envisioning what it would look like if you thrived on your work, rather than just survived. If you had the opportunity to jump ship and do something you love and get paid for it, would you take it? I know I did. When I quit my government consulting job to start *College Magazine*, I took a financial risk to follow my passion. In fact, I took a pay cut in the thousands my first year alone just to do so. #YOLO

Today, I run a six-figure business that continues to flourish. Without my passion fueling me along the way, I would have never achieved this success. This passion career ultimately brings me lifestyle *and* happiness wealth—like location flexibility and creative freedom—which is every bit as important to me as traditional wealth.

I'm not alone in sacrificing my high-paying job for my passion. Sarah Bidnick, now the senior vice president of marketing for Today-Tix, took a similar financial risk. She put aside her passion for film after graduating college because she didn't think it could be a viable career option. Instead, she worked the first six years of her career at JP Morgan Chase, moving into an assistant vice president position and earning a stellar salary well beyond many of her peers.

"I learned a ton [at JP Morgan Chase] but I knew the entire time that it wasn't really what I wanted to do for a living," said Sarah.

She sensed that the financial industry wasn't her calling, and wasn't feeling fulfilled. Sarah was willing to do whatever it took to follow her passion. Ultimately, she left her job to pursue a career in film.

Don't get me wrong, yes, there is definitely risk involved in jumping ship. Risk is necessary to bring great change in your life. But that doesn't mean you can't take smart risks, and there's no need to quit your job today without a plan.

Sarah didn't have any film experience to her name. "Every job I submitted for, I wouldn't even get a call." She took to Craigslist to find people who needed help on small film projects or needed a PA for the day and took any opportunity she could get. She started at the bottom at first. Key words: *at first*.

At these small gigs, Sarah spoke her passion and new opportunities presented themselves. "Every person that I met wanted to introduce me to the next person. If you're willing to show up, work really hard, and be clear about where it is you're trying to go, people want to help you get there," said Sarah.

That's how Sarah got her next job at Silverdocs, an American international film festival launched by the American Film Institute and the Discovery Channel, held in Silver Spring, Maryland.

"[Silverdocs] was probably the job that most aligned with my passion, that I still to this day have ever had. I met Academy Award-winning film directors, and got to introduce them on stages, and got to welcome crowds of thousands to see film that was just absolutely my favorite type of film."

It took guts to make that leap from a secure career path, but after gaining experience, she started working her way up in her passion industry. She's now the senior vice president of marketing at TodayTix, the mobile app for last-minute theater tickets. In fact, she's been with the startup since day one, helping grow TodayTix to 13 cities and raise more than $15MM in financing since 2013. Safe to say, her financial risk paid off in more than dollars.

At TodayTix, Sarah is deeply connected to the mission of the organization. Her job aligns with her passion for creative projects. Her position also allows her to lean on her strengths in analytics and data. She oversees five different departments, leading her teams in go-to-market strategy, user acquisition and performance marketing, customer retention and loyalty, partner marketing, and sales strategies. She tackles big questions like: *Which cities will TodayTix enter next? How will we improve the app? What's the best way to present our marketing metrics to the board?*

Sarah gets to fully embrace the TodayTix mission to redefine the way we see theater.

Will Hansen also took the leap. He left his steady-paying career in the military as a dental lab technician, abandoning the dental track completely to go to art school and become an interactive media designer. He desired to flex his creativity and love for minimalistic design.

"I've always been a creative at heart. Growing up, I was always drawing, I was always doing photography, I was always making films… writing poetry; anything to get that creativity out of me, I was doing it," said Will.

Will spent a decade in dentistry, studying dental prosthetics. He felt connected with the more artistic side of fabricating dentures, carving wax for crowns and bridges and making realistic implants. But when he sought to pursue dentistry further, he realized it wasn't the right fit.

"[Dentistry] isn't my passion; this isn't my path, and quite frankly I don't want to look in mouths the rest of my life," said Will.

Fueled by this realization and an excitement to pursue his love for art full time, Will took the risk of earning less money and started anew. "I think there's nothing to be ashamed of by following your heart and your gut."

Everything clicked for Will once he was on this new track. Starting from the bottom, both in title and pay, he began to build his network, interning and freelancing on small graphic design projects. He steadily grew in his field and is now in a successful career doing what he loves, as the experience design manager and visual product lead at Intuit on the TurboTax team. That's right—Will finds fun and creativity in doing your taxes. Imagine how many people Will impacts daily, supplying helpful feedback and creating a positive experience for his team of product designers while advancing a product that makes people's lives easier.

Yes, it's true: All these intelligent people, in high-paying leadership positions, got to where they are by taking a risk—missing out on higher salaries and steady trajectories all in the name of passion.

If you're early in your career journey, you may be in luck and won't need to abandon your income to pursue your passion. If you're already in the workforce, know that sometimes taking a pay cut is crucial, but it will pay off eventually.

Hold the phone. This doesn't mean you should quit your job today, especially if you rely on your steady paycheck for your expenses. We all have different circumstances, such as crippling student debt or family members who need caretaking, and it's impossible to give a one-size-fits-all answer on when to make the leap.

Remember, it's a marathon, not a sprint. You don't have to risk it for the biscuit right now. You can slow your roll and begin by volunteering in the field of your dreams, working a side hustle, or joining organizations that relate to your passion. You can practice your skills and gain experience until you feel comfortable enough, both emotionally and financially, to take the next step of exploring your passion full-time.

Even now, I am not working as a full-time author. I'm sitting in Lestats, a 24/7 coffee shop in San Diego, writing at 9:00 p.m. on a Saturday. I know what you're thinking, and you're right. Yes, I'd rather be binge-watching Riverdale. But when you're passionate about something, like I am, you make it happen. Cheryl and her bold red lip can wait.

A passion career journey is just that: a journey. This is the long game. Don't be in a rush or pressure yourself to achieve everything all at once. (I know, easier said than done. Let this be your mantra as you take action on each step of your intentional career journey.)

"I'm finding the younger the employee is, the more stress they have around where they think they are today and where they should be," explained Christine DiDonato, founder of Career Revolution and AwesomeBoss.com. The key word is "should be." When our expectations of achievement don't match up to the reality, that's a recipe for disappointment. That's like expecting to design your entire bullet journal to perfection after watching just one YouTube tutorial.

I'll admit, I'm not always the best at taking my own advice about the journey. I'd love to snap my fingers and have this book published as we speak. But I knew logically that if I stayed committed and wrote one thousand words a day for three months, that the book would materialize.

And if you're reading this, it worked. #lifegoals

Pa$$ion pays

Passion will always win.

What do I mean by this? Passionate people are more likely to get a job than people whose passions do not align with the organization.

Take it from our girl Christine DiDonato. As a former head of talent management at Sony Electronics, Christine focuses her passion and research on developing young employees to be the next generation of leaders.

"When you show excitement about something, it comes through without you having to fake it," said Christine. She explained that when we share our passions and the ways in which we've explored them, we can't help but show up as genuine.

Simply put, companies are hiring you beyond your qualifications. They're hiring you for your authentic passion. Christine has hired for and worked with 1-percent brands including PlayStation, Hulu, and DollarShaveClub. If the 1-percent brands care about authenticity, the 99-percent brands (smaller brands or simply brands you may not be familiar with) care too.

Passion is your differentiator, that secret ingredient employers seek. Want proof? In 2019, Unsplash, one of my favorite sites for free stock images, posted an ad for a community specialist. The job description read: "We are looking for individuals who are community-oriented and passionate about the open photography movement." They actually used the word "passion" in their description. *Kismet?* I think not.

The description went on to list specific tangible aspects of the position, such as executing growth campaigns and programs, working with social media, and supporting company-wide marketing launches. Yes, these skill sets are important, but they are not the be-all end-all—anyone could have these skills. The key to the ideal candidate lies in the words— written in the posting *above* any technical requirements, "communi- ty-oriented and passionate about the open photography movement."

Imagine that you are applying for a position with Unsplash in social media marketing. You are a very skilled user of social media, a self-proclaimed influencer if you will. You have a degree in marketing, plus past experience building an online community at your summer gig. But there's another candidate. Lisa has the exact same education and experience, *but* in her free time, she travels to national parks, takes photos of landscapes, and sends them to the parks to use on their website for free. Who do you think will get the job?

Obvi, it's Lisa! She has clearly and tangibly demonstrated her passion for the open photography movement. You might both get the interview, but Lisa gushes about her photography project and the excitement of the Mission Trails Regional Park team when they received her photos free of charge.

This connection between Lisa's passion and the mission of the company is what makes all the difference. Passion. Always. Wins. Period.

Remember Sarah from TodayTix? She hires dozens of young professionals in their 20s for their fast-growing startup. When she speaks about hiring, she focuses on applicants' passions.

"One of the things that's always really impressive is having been involved in a lot of different things that they're passionate about. Especially if they are things that they created...on their own or with a small group of people... It shows a lot of initiative and the fact that they're not afraid to try something new or get involved," said Sarah.

Even if there isn't an open position available at TodayTix, Sarah still prioritizes passion. "I've had young people really voice a specific interest or desire to be affiliated with TodayTix in one way or another. And when they're excited enough about it and willing to show up and try a bunch of different things, then we find a way to fit them in," said Sarah.

Yes, you read that right: Even if there's not an open position currently listed, you should still reach out and connect with companies that align with your passion. "At least 70 percent, if not 80 percent, of jobs are not published," said Matt Youngquist, the president of Career Horizons Career Coaching in an interview with NPR.[4]

Otherwise speaking, if you're seeking your passion career, the way in is likely not listed on job boards. Your time is better spent networking and speaking directly to employers like Sarah than scouring sites for the newest listings.

If I had it my way, there would be high school and college courses dedicated to helping young people discover their passion. Why is it that when you said you were passionate about art, you heard the fear-mongering phrase "starving artist" instead of "let your passion inspire your career journey"? Imagine all the art-related careers out there, and how you could have reached them if someone had encouraged you to follow your passion, instead of minimizing it as a hobby.

Why does it seem that adults tend to crush young people's creative dreams instead of helping them connect the dots to the many creative careers that exist in the world? I personally believe it is because many people haven't gone after their own dreams and passions, so they can't see how it is feasible. Maybe they think they are protecting young people from failure. Maybe they know how challenging following your passion can be, and they want to protect young people from taking on something too difficult. But you're not just any young person, you're YOU. You are not afraid of a challenge. If you are anything like me in my first job out of college, you're bored with work and you are *craving* a challenge.

At nine years old, Sarah adored making movies. She remembers creating her first video for her parents set to music in 1998, years before the accessible movie-making tools of iMovie. But after college graduating from the University of Scranton with a B.S. in Finance, she felt the societal pressure to stay the course and chose the practical career working as an analyst for an elite investment bank.

When Sarah decided to leave, she leaned on her passion for movie making as her differentiator, and worked her way up in the industry. At one point she connected to a marketing and distribution position with OURsceneTV, a video lifestyle channel for the LGBTQ+ community. This opportunity felt serendipitous, but in all actuality, it can be attributed to Sarah speaking her passion. This position even involved behind-the-camera work on the red carpet, leading interviews with celebrities like Lady GaGa.

From there, Sarah combined her love of media with her craving for structure and data from her finance background into the advertising and media space, working at The Fearless Group, a full-service advertising and communication agency in New York. Oftentimes when you get creative, people can connect a seemingly straightforward or dry subject such as finance to something exciting. In this case, Sarah used her finance background as her differentiator on her passion track to connect to her career at TodayTix.

The key point of this journey is not in the end moment of the journey. It's the intentional steps along the way, working for companies that align with your passion. In her career Sarah worked on small projects and for companies that you've probably never heard of. And that's okay, that's what a passion career journey often looks like.

Let me break it down for you: Most companies and brands you know have hundreds of employees. Yet there are more than 14 million companies in North America with less than 50 employees.[5] 14 million! Compare that to less than 300,000 companies that have 50 to 1,000-plus employees. Can you see how it's very likely that you haven't heard of most companies?

I'll never forget when I was eleven years old and I first tried—*wait for it*—bacon. Yes, I hadn't ever tasted that delicious, oil-dripping, savory meat-compliment to eggs. I grew up in a predominantly Jewish town and because many people around me kept kosher I wasn't ever exposed to it. It wasn't until I made friends with a Christian girl and her family cooked me bacon that I got my first bite. Naturally, I was hooked.

Swap bacon with any other food you've tried for the first time. Consider that overjoyed feeling of *oh, I never knew about that!* That's what it's like when you discover careers that you had no idea existed. No matter how stable you feel in your life, you can always be surprised and have unexpected adventures along the way. You can try gelato for the first time while abroad in Italy and wonder how that tasty treat had been hiding from you all your life. Or you can go out and proactively start looking for your favorite flavor today.

In other words, it's okay to stumble upon new foods. But don't stumble into your career.

When you rely on only the companies you know exist, you feel that you must work for these big, and often very competitive brands. It's time to get over the idea that the path to a fulfilling career is to work for a big-brand company. These companies make up such a small percentage of the great places to work.

Andrea Stone also integrated her passion for art into her career and worked for smaller organizations she had never heard of before. Like Sarah, Andrea's path was nonlinear, beginning in a completely different field as a criminology and sociology double major at the University of Maryland. In fact, she admitted to originally choosing the majors without much intention other than avoiding a public speaking course requirement. She graduated in 2006 and felt unsure of what she wanted to do.

After college, Andrea decided to apply for a program to gain teaching experience, on the path to what she felt was her passion: becoming a school counselor. She taught special education classes for one year at an inner-city school in Baltimore but felt overwhelmed. She ended up ditching her job at the end of the year, reconsidering her passion and switching paths entirely, working in a recruiting position for an IT consulting company.

But she knew she was capable of so much more. She didn't see herself sitting at a desk all day on a computer anymore. When she received an offer letter for another desk job, she realized she had to finally take the leap to follow her original passion. She went on to earn her Master of Education and Master of Psychological Counseling degrees in order to become a school counselor.

Today, Andrea has connected her enthusiasm for mental health, her passion for helping young people build upon their social skills, and her love for art into a career as an elementary school counselor for two schools in Paramus, New Jersey. Andrea uses art regularly as an interactive tool in her lessons with her students.

Every day is different for Andrea, teaching character education lessons, holding small social groups, and helping her students solve their conflicts. Meanwhile, she instills creativity in a new generation.

"I think we are so in this mindset that if we know what we want, we expect it to come immediately, and it should be a very straight line to our goal, but it's all over the place and it does take a while, and I know for me there was so much doubt along the way," she said.

Andrea exemplifies the journey to discover what feeds your soul and intentionally integrate it into your dream career.

Rachel Aldrich used her passion as her differentiator in achieving her dream career. She knew she was passionate about reading and words from a young age but had trouble finding a job she enjoyed. As a recent graduate from Boston College, Rachel began her career journey in 2016 as a finance and technology reporter. But she quickly discovered that churning out articles on Apple stocks didn't fit so well with her passion.

"It's really hard to find your passion and what you want to devote every day to. It's okay if you go out and you get a job and it's not something you love. It's totally fine to pivot," said Rachel."

She reached out to her network, simply connecting with friends who had jobs she thought were interesting, and made her next move. Rachel found that even distant acquaintances were willing to help her out.

She's now an assistant marketing manager at Penguin Random House, the publishing company, where she works on marketing campaigns with authors for their upcoming books. Rachel gets to write ad copy, develop creative online strategies, and work on book promotions to help her authors' book launches succeed, all while spreading her love for reading and ideas.

Sarah, Andrea, and Rachel all achieved their passion careers because they took the time to recognize, listen to, and take action on their passions.

The doors to their passion careers opened because each of them intentionally followed what they loved. If there's one message you remember from this book, it's that passion always wins. That's because when you speak your passion, doors open.

It's never too late to follow your passion—even if you've been in your career for years and are no longer passionate about your work. Remember Sarah and Will? They started to explore their passions five to ten years after establishing themselves in completely different fields. And they're not the exception; they're the rule. More people than you think have shifted careers.

In fact, according to the Bureau of Labor Statistics, the average person changes their job 12 times in their career.[6] Twelve times! In the Bureau's January 2018 report, the average employee tenure at a job was 4.2 years.[7] Just remember, if you want to change jobs, you are not alone.

Living in a zombie world

Seriously ask yourself, when's the last time you paused to think about what you like to do? In fact, when's the last time you stopped to reflect on your life in general?

Really take a minute here to think about this. Did you take 20 minutes this week to stop what you were doing and reflect on your life and goals? If you can't answer this with conviction, chances are you're meandering through life like a Zombie. #JusticeforGlenn

If you haven't taken this time, do it now.

More often than not, we're just going through the motions. According to a study in 2017 commissioned by Marks & Spencer, 96 percent of 3,000 people surveyed said they were living life on autopilot.[8] In the study they asked about decisions such as what to wear in the morning, meals and weekend plans. That means we're making unconscious decisions—sleepwalking through our lives.

This disposition of non-engagement with our environment and our decision-making may seem innocent at first glance. But imagine an entire lifetime of this approach and the negative influence it can have on our career journey.

I think we can all agree that it's much easier to live like we're sleepwalking, following our same patterns and habits. That causes us to tread water, remain stagnant, and thus see little progress. And we can't achieve something different if we're doing the same ole' same ole', can we? Absolutely not.

When was the last time you worked on something meaningful to you? Furthermore, when was the first time you took action to make it happen? And no, I don't mean the twenty minutes you spent last night scrolling through your Instagram feed to like puppy photos and updating your Hinge profile. (Not judging, just saying!)

Few people try to intentionally create a career experience that they'll love because it's hard work. But I can personally say, having sat in dozens of yawn-inducing meetings at a job that I didn't like, staying in a field you don't care about is even harder. Don't let years pass you by as you work in a career you don't love because TBH that's the real hard work—pretending to be fulfilled and accepting that this is all life has in store for you.

If you put in the intentional hustle to follow your passion career, the results, though slow at first, will start to come easy. You will see the *cue mystical music* Law of Attraction working for you—you'll overflow with passion, spreading it and speaking it, and connect to the opportunities that feed your hangry soul.

The Law of Attraction is a belief that our thoughts, whether negative or positive, will manifest experiences. In other words, you attract the intentions you put out in the world. Some may interpret the Law of Attraction as a request to the universe, but the way I see it, and have experienced it working, is a manifestation that occurs because we create intentional action around those thoughts.

Only when you take the time to reflect will you unlock your passion. Julie Reisler, CEO of Empowered Living, encourages us to trust our inner voice. "Notice what gives you energy. Follow the breadcrumbs that are going to leave clues to what you love." But how can you listen to your inner voice if you haven't taken the time to shut up and hear that voice speak? Take out your Air Pods and listen to what your inner voice has to say; you might be surprised.

It sounds corny, but it's true! I could gush about *College Magazine* all damn day. On the other hand, I could only complain to you about my old job because trying to portray it in a positive light would feel painful, and insincere.

Before you keep reading, set up a concrete time to focus exclusively on your passion. Treat this exercise like a job interview. Schedule a time on your calendar. That's right, a passion career meeting with yourself! Even a single meeting is one step closer toward uncovering your passion and connecting it to your career.

Newsflash! Did you know that if you actually write down and schedule a time and place where you're going to make something happen, like unlocking your passion, you are more likely to do just that? "Deciding in advance when and where you will take specific actions to reach your goal can double or triple your chances for success," according to Heidi Grant Halvorson, social psychologist, speaker, and author who studies the science of motivation and communication.

So, mark your calendar for 30 minutes to an hour. Open up that dusty planner that you just had to have and finally put it to good use. Taking the time to pause, reflect, and visualize is so important. It's time to prioritize your passion and start getting intentional.

2

WILL YOU TEACH ME
EVERYTHING?

Before we can uncover your passion, we need to create space for the idea of a passion career. In other words, invite with open arms the very possibility that you can connect your passion to a career.

Otherwise, you may have difficulty taking action on your passion career because you'll feel skeptical about the journey. The passion career journey is dripping with possibility—and you need to embrace the idea of endless opportunities.

Possibility is a mindset, the way you see things. And most likely, your current mindset is stuck at what I like to call a "blank slate": You feel that you have a lot to learn but not so much to offer. Let me explain:

College graduation, or whatever the last step of your education was (high school, associate degree, graduate school, etc.), feels like a steep cliff. Each year of your education, you put in work and climb to new heights, reaching higher elevations than you thought possible. You even figure out how to use that pickaxe along the way. Now imagine that pickaxe is CAD software, statistical analysis tools, writing techniques, or public-speaking practices that completely confused you when you first heard of them. It may have baffled you at first, but you conquered them. Then at graduation, you leap off into the real world.

Maybe you have a parachute, like Mom and Dad, to soften the blow of your landing. Or maybe you've invested in repelling gear, like that part-time barista job. Or maybe, like many graduates, you dive into a free fall.

If you feel like this, you are not alone.

In fact, only 34% of students believe they will graduate with the skills and knowledge to be successful in the job market, according to Gallup's 2017 College Student Survey of 32,000 students.[9]

That remaining 66% of graduates, who feel they won't graduate with the skills and knowledge, simply do not feel confident in their abilities or don't know how to connect them to a career. I'd argue that any perceived deficiency is rooted in a lack of intentional career planning. IMO, I do not believe these graduates lack skills; they lack *confidence*.

That lack of confidence and anxiety about life after graduation stems from "blank slate syndrome." A blank slate means that you see yourself as waiting to be molded into the person you want to be.

A blank slate is like a newborn in the real world. You're curious and eager to learn the lessons of corporate life, but you feel you have nothing to offer…so rather than trying to learn, you ugly cry every time you get stuck. This is a lackadaisical approach that keeps you from taking control of your future. No one, and I mean *no one*, wants to hire a blank slate.

For example, Becca saw herself as a blank slate after college. She had no idea what she was going to do. She started applying to every job she came across, no matter the field. In interviews, Becca tried to guess what the interviewers wanted to hear and didn't really have a grasp on where she wanted to be in a year or two. Guess what?

She didn't get any of those jobs. Shocker. No matter what you may think now, you are not a blank slate and graduation is not a metaphorical cliff.

Upon graduation, your expertise continues to grow to new heights as you continue to climb upward on your career journey. Even if your current career doesn't align with what you desire for your passion career, the skill sets and experiences you're developing now are more transferable than you think.

Despite the headlines calling today's graduates the "entitled generation," I don't believe that recent graduates or young professionals expect perfect careers to land in their laps. I have worked with hundreds of college students, and more often people can't help but be swayed by this messaging. In other words, the result is the opposite of entitled—feeling unworthy.

I hear it again and again: *I'm not good enough. I'm not qualified. I chose the wrong major.*

For recent grads venturing into the workforce, that feeling of doubt creeps in almost immediately. Even before graduating, leading up to graduating knowing that you're approaching the cliff's edge. A single job rejection letter (or from simply not hearing back) only fuels doubt's fire. Suddenly you feel like you don't have control over what happens with your future because you can't fathom what it will look like. You start to fear that you'll be stuck, miserable, or simply settling for mediocrity in your future career.

Why do you feel this way? Perhaps it's because the structure of academia suddenly disappears beneath your feet. Your entire life up to this point has revolved around school, so, of course, it's going to feel scary and weird when you leave and have no predetermined routine or direction. In the words of Gretchen Wieners, you thought it would be so *fetch* to join the real world, but instead it's not all rainbows and unicorns.

You don't know a world without syllabi, professors, exam dates, university calendars, and the comfort of grade levels. Or, you may have trouble visualizing what the real world expects from you. It's understandable that you don't feel prepared. It's reasonable to think you'll need to start at the very bottom, with the cliché image of fetching coffee for your boss while you learn the real-world skills of email etiquette and communication. (But maybe take *Devil Wears Prada* with a grain of salt.) If you're changing career paths, you may feel that you're unqualified and have nothing to offer—and that your work should be relegated to basic tasks.

But all of this is a myth.

When I applied to my first job at a government consulting firm, I felt a serious learning curve quickly approaching. Until that point, I didn't really have anything substantial to offer in a job like professional consulting.

However, did I go into my interview as a blank slate? Absolutely not! OMG could you imagine?

"Hey, I'm here for that one interview. I have no idea what to expect. Can you define what government consulting means exactly? K thanks."

If you project your fear of the unknown, you'll look clueless. Obviously, I felt anxiety over what the job would be like. But did I let that feeling consume me and prevent me from putting my best Chelsea boot forward? No way. Did I let the fact that I didn't hear back from three other consulting firms I applied to stand in my way? Absolutely not.

The mystery around the job itself—not to mention the idealistic job description asking for 40-plus qualifications and 10 years of experience—can cause so much fear that it halts you from even applying. That's where it is absolutely essential to remind yourself: You are not a blank slate.

In actuality, your academic skills, volunteer/internship positions, and early career experiences are more transferable than you think. Kari

Gold, senior HR operations partner at the Association of American Medical Colleges (AAMC), has 10 years of experience hiring young professionals.

"If employers are looking for someone who has supervised someone before, if you've led a project, or have been part of a large team where you've had some big responsibilities—to me that's supervising. It may not be direct supervising, but it still applies," said Kari.

Translation: You are more qualified than you realize.

There's no way you graduated from college, or even high school, without the dreadful experience of a team project. Good thing though because team projects are literally how work gets done in companies.

MacGyver that ish

But what if my degree or past experiences don't align with what I'm passionate about? What if I want a career in computer engineering, but I have never written a line of code in my life?

That's A-OK. First, recognize the experiences you *do* have that connect to your passion. This approach will get you closer to a qualified mindset—where you start to see all of the ways in which you are qualified instead of all the ways in which you feel you may fall short.

Perhaps you're great at math and aced your statistics course with ease. Perhaps you're a pro when it comes to attention to detail, which can be seen in how you organize your notes. What about that video design class you took that required elements of coding?

These are all examples from one of the students I tutor at Reality Changers named Gedle Gedleh, a senior at Helix High School in San Diego. He's paving his path toward a career in computer engineering. At first, he felt like he wasn't really qualified, after all, he was just 17 and he hadn't taken a formal coding class…that is, until we uncovered all these related experiences.

"My dad used to be a computer engineer, and when I saw [his work], I just knew I always wanted to be a computer engineer. I like the idea of making something that people would enjoy and would help them support their lives for the better. I think I'd like to be part of creating technology that people need in hospitals," said Gedle.

Gedle's story and experience are unique to him and will set him apart from anyone seeking a career in computer engineering. By following his passion and building upon this foundation of relevant experiences, Gedle will continue to create an intentional journey towards his passion career. Go Gedle, go!

Your passion can fuel your journey toward the career you want. The key is to see it as a journey and know that you'll need to start creating intentional experiences around this passion today.

Does that mean that if you're like Gedle, looking to break into the computer engineering field, you need to join a fancy, expensive coding class? Absolutely not. But could you join a WordPress Meetup group in your city? Could you participate in your school's computer engineering club? Could you watch a YouTube video each night on how to code and then blog about what you learn? Yes, yes, and YASSS.

All of these steps will better your ability to stand out when you start applying for jobs and making important networking connections.

Honestly, that blog you started can serve as a tangible expression of your passion. When you learn something new, reflect on it, and write it down in the form of something like a blog, you gain a stronger understanding of the subject. Not to mention, you're building your personal brand. By sharing what you learn and teaching it to others, you are more likely to benefit from the information.

"Sharing what I learn in different contexts to different audiences [gives] me a chance to internalize the lessons; I do that primarily through writing," said Dan Casetta, a transformational leader for 30 years in the Vector Marketing/Cutco sales organization and business coach. He also spreads his influence through writing, speaking and hosting gatherings of like-minded, success-oriented people.

Blogging or working on a portfolio project over time shows your devotion to your passion. Instead of waiting a week before a job interview to start the blog, start today. Even if it's just a small step—like one post per month, a photo per week, or a subpar clip of you practicing the JLo Dance Challenge. It doesn't matter if anyone reads your blog in the beginning; all that matters is that you took your passion a step further and contributed to building your personal brand online.

But what if my degree isn't related to my passion career? This is a common question among students who attend liberal arts colleges. Most people that choose to study philosophy or political science or Africana studies don't necessarily plan to be philosophers, politicians, or professors. But in these fields of study, students learn critical thinking, persuasive writing, and public speaking abilities along with many other valuable skills. Coupled with the intentional experiences the students seek out when going to school for these majors, these fields of study make them exceptional candidates for endless career possibilities.

Take Laurence Jackson, for example. He knew he was passionate about film from the get-go. He started creating films with a digital camcorder when he was 14 years old, but he had decided to attend his state university, University of Maryland, which didn't offer a film major.

Instead of accepting that he wouldn't be able to pursue his passion at school, he took that as an opportunity to create his own path and launch a film society on campus. He wrote and directed a feature film called *Hollow* his freshman year.

The movie had a message for college students who were struggling to find their way. After debuting the film at Maryland's theater, Laurence was flown out to the University of California, Irvine to show the film there too. One student voiced that he saw himself in the film and it made him realize he didn't know who he was but that he wanted to figure it out. Hearing that feedback left a serious impression on Laurence.

"I think that changed my life. Because...that was what I wanted to do with film and for the first time I got a little bit of, *it's possible.*"

Laurence knew he wanted to continue to write and make films that would make a difference. It's no surprise that today he works on the Netflix Original Series *You* and produces SAG short films on the side.

So, what you're saying is if I want to work for a publishing company but I've never been a strong writer or I don't have experience getting published, I can still pursue that career? Yes, 100 percent.

Kick it off today. Start writing. Start joining. You can start taking action immediately when you determine and declare your passion. If you wait to take action, you resist your future. Don't hesitate on taking the next steps that will move you closer to what you love.

Maybe you should pick another sport

But what if the opportunity I want is too competitive? Maybe I'm not a blank slate, but am I strong enough to get this top-notch position?

Yes, again!

Sometimes we get the impression that were not good enough to make the team. The key here is patience and growth over time. Laurence didn't just walk onto the Warner Brothers lot and get handed the job. He spent years creating a foundation of intentional experiences working toward his passion career, starting with less competitive opportunities.

In order to uncover those less competitive opportunities, you'll want to understand the difference between linear and nonlinear careers. Linear careers are where you follow one specific track and advance in that track. Meanwhile, nonlinear careers take varied routes and expose you to diverse fields. As a result, linear careers will likely be more competitive than nonlinear careers because they're the more obvious routes. Nonlinear careers are often less competitive and a excellent place to gain experience.

For example, if you love soccer and you want to be a professional soccer player, that's a linear career path. But only 2% of NCAA student-athletes go on to be professional athletes.[10] Talk about competitive AF!

I'm not saying you shouldn't chase after your dreams of being the next Cristiano Ronaldo, but it's important to acknowledge competitive passions. If your playing isn't on fleek enough to join a professional club, you can still connect that passion for soccer to a similar career.

This doesn't just mean that your only other career option is to be a soccer coach. It means that you should consider *all* the organizations in the world that connect to soccer—like soccer media (podcasts, blogs, magazines, television), soccer reporting and broadcasting, soccer events, soccer stadiums, soccer equipment, soccer nonprofits, soccer swag, soccer technology, soccer talent agents, websites and social media dedicated to soccer...and the list goes on.

Imagine if your love for soccer could still be a part of your life on the daily. Even if you didn't go pro, you would feel fulfilled. Right?

You can still achieve competitive and coveted careers, but this doesn't happen instantaneously. Eva Gardner, the bassist for P!nk, didn't simply declare her passion for music and get recruited to tour with a Grammy Award-winning pop artist. She had a career journey just like you, which, through hard work and determination led her to one of the most competitive career opportunities.

"It all starts with starting. Playing in bands, playing at every club in L.A. that I could, being in every show that I could, and just being part of the scene and the community and the networking, and building the network," said Eva.

Eva recognized she was passionate about playing the bass since she was a child. Her dad also played the bass, and she looked up to him. She started pursing that passion by rehearsing daily, majoring in ethnomusicology at UCLA and showing up ready to play at just about any gig imaginable. Progress, progress, progress.

"When you put yourself out there and you play with other people, they see how you work—work ethic is a really big thing, whether you're playing to two people in a club to two hundred to two thousand, you should be playing the same show," said Eva.

You don't make it to the top 1 percent of the most competitive opportunities overnight. You have to buckle down and put in the work. Don't give up a dream just because it's competitive without even exploring the nonlinear and related opportunities. Just because you don't think you'll make it to Broadway doesn't mean you can't work in the theater industry like Sarah Bidnick at TodayTix.

Even though something is competitive, that doesn't mean you don't deserve it and that you can't achieve it; it just means you may have a longer journey towards it.

And don't get caught up comparing yourself to the people we see on television, working on 1-percent careers, who make success look easy. They worked hard too, and sometimes they were simply in the right place at the right time. There's nothing wrong with that. But if you compare your first steps to someone else's one hundredth step, you'll discourage yourself before you even begin to take action.

Remember our guy Will Hansen? After graduating from the Art Institute, he wanted to work at a creative agency and be a leader in the design industry, creating websites and designs that millions of people would utilize. He started out with a small freelance job that paid him $100 to make a website. Today he's one of the lead graphic designers behind Intuit's TurboTax website that does, in fact, reach hundreds of millions. It didn't happen overnight—it was a career journey.

In each of these cases, even the most competitive careers can only be achieved with the right mindset of possibility. The mindset that, given enough time, you can figure out how to get anywhere you want to go. The mindset that you can learn and achieve a career that you are passionate about and fulfilled by. Because it's true.

Take me, for instance. Even though I could barely imagine what a job as a consultant would be like, I felt confident in my own ability to cross that bridge when I got there. You should feel confident in that too.

At your very core, you know you are capable of learning just about anything, and that's the tea.

I knew I had a lot to offer as a recent graduate, no matter what the job. All I needed to do was communicate my passions effectively. Challenge accepted.

During my interview for my first consulting position, I spoke about a consulting project that I had worked on my junior year for Baltimore Gas & Electric (BG&E) to reduce energy consumption in their offices.

As I sat down with the hiring team, I walked them through each step of my experience—how my class project team and I formulated questions for the client, conducted survey research of the employees, and developed three actionable solutions based on our research, one of which was swapping out the light fixtures with high-efficiency bulbs. I spoke about my abilities to develop a report of our findings, present them to the client, and deliver implementable solutions to help them reduce energy use.

Now reflect on your own projects that you have been a part of and consider how you can tell that story.

Think about that time you had to present an argument on gun control for your English class. You started out knowing nothing about the current laws on gun control but by the end, you were well-versed enough to form a strong and persuasive opinion. Or consider that one-year project where you learned about poetry and created your own book of poems? These experiences are your proof that you can start from scratch and learn just about anything.

By communicating my experiences and my passion for consulting (working on a challenging problem, getting creative, and devising a measured solution), I got the job. And prior to that, I networked by attending my school's career fair and built a meaningful connection with one of the company's recruiters who I knew from an intentional program I was part of. Efforts like these all help you in achieving your career goals.

"Too cutthroat" is just an excuse. #SorryNotSorry. Take on the less competitive opportunities and work your way up to competitive careers.

Blank slate blues

Are you suffering from the blank slate blues? If so, it's time to get well because I have a secret for you...AHEM: You aren't a blank slate. You are a multifaceted career strategist with unlimited information to offer. Yes, that's right—YOU! Should I say it louder for the people in the back?

Everything you've learned up to this point has contributed to your knowledge foundation and skill set. And I mean *everything*.

These experiences might include selling handmade string bracelets on the playground in fifth grade; the after-school babysitting gig with three unruly boys; the barista shift at Starbucks; the variety show fundraiser you organized in high school; the Greek Life "Fraternity Men of Maryland" calendar you created as part of your sorority's philanthropy project.

All these experiences are part of *my* career story. I bet you have a list just as fun, quirky, and varied as mine. And within your experiences is a common thread—YOU! Your ideas, your dedication, your impact, your leadership, your potential.

Life experiences are part of your career story. A career is simply where you put your life skills into action as you participate in the real-world economy (production, distribution, and consumption of goods and services) and work toward your organization or company's mission, as well as your own personal career vision.

The industry you're looking to enter is not some big mystery that can only be tackled once you arrive. Simply consider all the knowledge, energy and passion you have to offer.

Just imagine yourself in the shoes of your employer (fingers crossed they aren't Crocs). She is probably in her 40s or 50s, at least 20 years out of college; just don't remind her of that. Her passion and energy have been tested like my patience with the group project slacker.

She's looking for fresh eyes. *You* are those fresh eyes. You embody the passionate and talented energy the company seeks.

It's feasible to assume you understand the newest technologies, the latest research from your classes. Best of all, you understand what they fear most but need desperately for their brand: the power of social media.

There are just two problems: You think you're a blank slate and you're not quite sure about this whole passion thing. That's OK. That's why you're reading this book.

I'm here to help you shift your mindset and help you realize everything you have to offer. I'm here to help you shape that very true story around your passion. Together, we'll create a career strategy that aligns with your interests, strengths, and values and helps you achieve your dream career.

No, you're not about to fall off that metaphorical cliff—the only thing that should make that plunge is the doubt you harbor that you are not qualified enough, and the Crocs that your hypothetical employer is sporting at the office.

Because what does it mean to be qualified anyways? Don't unqualified people get the job all the time...?

According to a report by Hewlett Packard, women feel they need to meet 100% of job criteria before applying— every bullet point on that job description. And LinkedIn's data reflects this stat: Women are applying to 20% fewer jobs than men.[11] This means that we each interpret qualified differently.

Here's the thing, unfortunately, feeling unqualified can become a vicious cycle. As you grow up, you gain more experience, but it's never enough for what's next. But it doesn't have to be this way. Feeling qualified is the act of continually climbing the mountain, building your skill set over time.

Look back at where you were five years ago and think about how much you've grown and all the new experience you've had. You've done it before and you will continue to grow.

No matter where you are in life—high school, beginning college, senior year, finishing a graduate degree, or already in your professional career—let's take a step back and discover what you're passionate about so you can continue hustling.

3

WHO AM I?

P assion is what ignites you to get out of your oh-so comfy bed in the morning. Passion is the desire that brightens your soul. Passion is the element that attracts others to you.

Simply put, your passion is what makes you *you*. You can't fake passion because it's an authentic force that comes from within. When you convey your passion, you become memorable.

Passion shouldn't be a scary word, stop hitting "remind me later" out of fear. It's not like you're making a declaration that you are physically bound to, like a mortgage, marriage or a mediocre first tattoo. Passion can, and often does, evolve over time. And it's perfectly okay to feel that you may not have a passion. I'm here to challenge you to explore your interests, strengths, and values to help you discover your passion (or passions—why just stick to one? Be greedy!).

When was the last time you asked yourself what you're passionate about? Or when did you last spend a technology-free hour to journal, meditate, and contemplate what you enjoy? We often forget to prioritize, let alone identify, what it is we're passionate about.

Natalie Janji, author of *The Miracle Morning for College Students* and TEDx Speaker, explains that students often get lost in the day-to-day of getting good grades and building up their resumes with student clubs and internships. "We're students from kindergarten, and we're going nonstop until college... But what we're losing along the way is just getting time to ourselves to get to know ourselves a little better," said Janji.

In fact, we often stress out and bog ourselves down trying to figure out what we want to do for a profession without truly considering what we enjoy. How can we determine what we want to do for 40 hours a week if we only have a limited awareness of the opportunities in the world? Not to mention if we haven't taken the time to further explore the unknown and all the possible careers that can connect with what we love.

Instead of letting time pass you by, hit the pause button right now. Today we are going to start identifying and prioritizing your passions.

Step 1:
Establish wtf you want to do

When I look back at my childhood, my passion for creativity and entrepreneurship was obvious even at a young age. At seven years old, I remember lugging a tote bag of Barbie dolls next door to my BFF Elisa's house to play an extensive game of, well, Barbie. We created plot lines in these doll's lives and had them act it out. We even wrote and performed a Barbie play.

Additionally, we invented a system of communication between our homes where we drew the letters of the alphabet and most common words on pieces of paper large enough to see from one house window to the next. Sure, we had telephones (only landlines back in 1993) but inventing our own secret form of communication was much more entertaining.

During the Trolls craze in third grade, I had amassed a collection of miniature trolls and realized these naked dolls could benefit from different outfits. Who couldn't? I created multicolored designs using clay—t-shirts, shorts, and bikinis—and brought the trolls into school to sell them to my classmates for a dollar each. From there I even propositioned a couple of my friends to accompany me in my project (which, from an outsider's perspective, could have easily been considered a startup business).

One way to think about your passion is to think back to yourself as a kid. Where did your childlike wonder lead you? What games did you play? How did you interact with your friends?

When uncovering your passion, start by examining your interests and the things you enjoy. It's as simple as that.

If you're finding this challenging, keep in mind that the activity or interest doesn't have to impress anyone. Channel your judgment-free mindset. Put aside any potential reactions from your parents or friends.

Truly allow yourself to keep this thought process and outcome to yourself. Otherwise you may end up filtering your passion based on society's pressure of what will make the most money. I personally stopped considering the option of an art career based on this very cliché advice. This time, turn off your inner editor and allow yourself to think freely.

As kids, we're often asked what we want to be when we grow up. Then that question evolves into what we plan to do with our degree. After a certain point, when people expect you to be getting "serious" about your career, you get strange looks or disparaging comments if you aren't able to spout off a list of buzzwords associated with your goals.

Have you ever felt this judgment before? It's because people may not be familiar with your career path—whereas they are much more familiar with linear careers, such as doctor, lawyer, or computer programmer.

With these buzzword careers they can easily understand how you provide value in the economy and turn that into a salary. But if you're inspired by something like grant writing or history, they don't often congratulate or encourage you on your career path. I bet that few conversations you've had up to this point have been encouraging, with people urging you to further seek out opportunities or expand your understanding of how many different types of jobs involve your passion. Think about what you love most. Consider something you could do for hours without noticing the time passing; like that time you wrote a screenplay over your winter break or created your own brownie recipe. This exercise might come easier to some, whereas others may struggle.

Determining your interests can be as simple as thinking about what you love to do on a daily basis, whether it's reading, playing video games, watching *Game of Thrones* on HBO, strumming your guitar to Radiohead, or simply planning international-themed dinners with your friends. Get specific.

Look around your room for inspiration. Maybe it's the *Wicked* poster on your wall that reminds you of your passion for musical theatre or your souvenir koala that reminds you of your love of travel.

Your interest could even be the video game you spent hours defeating that made you realize how much you love challenges or that you're passionate about the gaming world.

Remember, your passions do not have to impress anyone else.

A side note about passions
that sound too fun to be careers

This is a good time to ignore that little nagging voice you've heard over and over from "established" adults who say things like "video games are a waste of time." (OK Boomer.) Even a single Google search for gaming careers will show you there are career opportunities across a wide range of talents in the video game industry. Did you know that the average starting salary for a game designer is $60,000 in 2018 according to Gamedesigning.org?[12]

Pro Tip:

If you're passionate about video games, consider Googling the name of the company that created your favorite game. See if they offer internships. Then Google local video game production companies in your area.

There's no such thing as a silly passion. You can be passionate about the weather, for example—you look forward to storms and love following their paths. This doesn't mean you need to become a meteorologist. It simply means you've identified an activity that captures your attention. Later on, we'll discuss how you can connect this interest to a potential career, but for now just focus on the interest itself.

"Notice what gives you energy and where you feel sparked and that can be a clue. You could be an RA and decide, *I really love the whole world of coaching or working with people and helping them…* Pay attention to what you love to do—even outside of the academic curriculum," said Julie Reisler, a multi-time TEDx speaker, host of *The You-est You* Podcast and author of the *Get a PhD in You* book series.

Right now, try not to worry about navigating your interests and how you can integrate your passion into your future—all you need to do now is put your interests out into the universe by writing them down.

Perhaps your passion feels intangible, like helping others. These intangible passions can be seen through tangible actions. You may not realize it at first when you're helping a friend with their calculus homework, but the sense of pride and fulfillment you feel is a strong indicator that you're on the right track.

Are you involved in an organization that you absolutely love? For example, maybe you look forward to attending meetings for your fraternity. Maybe you love being involved with Hillel on your campus. Or maybe you were fond of setting up that Kickstarter page and raising money for Relay for Life. You can be passionate about these causes, your role in supporting the cause, or simply the event itself.

You can even be passionate about watching TV or YouTube. There's no wrong answer when it comes to passions. Consider taking a moment to narrow this down. Are you passionate about a running television series like *Grey's Anatomy*, or do you love catching episodes here and there of *Top Chef*? Could what you watch signal what you're passionate about? Or do you simply feel passionate about the media form itself? I think it's a safe bet that Shonda Rhimes along with screenwriters, producers, and videographers, for example, would say they are passionate about watching TV.

Everyone has distinctive passions. Remember, your interests are part of what makes you *you*. But personally, I often find that hearing others' stories helps me get a better picture of how to define my own. I'm going to share my passions to give you an example of what a passion list may look like.

I'm passionate about helping you on your career journey. I enjoy reading, especially non-fiction, like *The Boy Who Harnessed the Wind* by William Kamkwamba and Bryan Mealer, and books on entrepreneurship, like *The E-Myth Revisited* by Michael E. Gerber. I love writing, especially about travel. I savor the moments journaling, traveling, surfing, and creating photo books of my adventures. I can't get enough of Maryland blue crabs, lobster, ramen, hotpot from Beijing, Shanghai soup dumplings, healthy dishes, and trying new international cuisines—food may be one of the biggest motivators in my life. (Where are all my self-declared foodies at?) I love creating new systems to make my life more efficient. I also look forward to taking my dog to Coronado dog beach.

I know my passion list is substantial, but that's because I've had a lot of time to think about my interests. It's totally cool if your passion list is just one thing or even one hobby. However, if you are like me and you also have a lot that you're passionate about, that's great too. The more passions you have, the more you can be able to align one or even a few of them with your future career.

Keep in mind, though, that interests change and evolve as we grow throughout different life stages. Our interests can be influenced over time by friends, family, teachers, and mentors. And we experience situational changes in our life circumstances—such as location, time, and income—that can have an effect, too.

One situational change for me was moving to San Diego, California. When I lived in Baltimore, Maryland—a three-hour drive away from the nearest surf-friendly ocean—who knew that I would fall in love with surfing? Yet here I am, 27 years later, after moving to California, taking any opportunity that comes my way to grab my surfboard and head out to sea.

If you're struggling to find a place to start, take some inspiration from the passion lists of students I've worked with over the years:

▸ "Helping others in any way I can, in any kind of forum," said Alexandra Blackwell, a media and communication studies student at Florida State University. She's also passionate about musical theatre and any tunes that she can sing along with or dance to. Not to mention exercise, as she uses anything from strength training to a sunrise salutation to challenge herself.

▸ Destine Manson, a student at New York University, is passionate about writing and using the power of words to incite change or to offer a different point of view. "Lastly, I have always had a passion for dance as an artistic outlet," said Destine.

▶ "Storytelling and ensuring that people have their [stories] told," said Sydney Foster, a film studies and production major at the University of Denver. She also enjoys being a steward for the environment and other species.

▶ Jennifer Croy, an English major at the University of Florida, is passionate about music, specifically singing and playing guitar. She enjoys developing her writing skills and then helping others develop those same skills. She also cares strongly about creating intentional relationships with her family and friends.

You may relate to some of these passions, or your list may be completely different. Either way, that's okay. I think you get the point. Passion can be anything and everything.

ACTION:

Visualization

In attending my first Best Year Ever Blueprint event—a community-created experience to help you have the best year of your life—I was coached through a visualization process. I was asked to close my eyes and visualize what I love.

For me, the process was transformational. I imagined myself on stage speaking to young women and elected officials about achieving a qualified mindset as a part of the 50by2050 Project, a recent initiative I launched through College Magazine. The 50by2050 Project, in partnership with Ignite National, Emily's List, Emerge America, Human Rights Campaign, Higher Heights, She Should Run, Victory Fund, and Running Start, engages college-aged women to start their political careers today in order to reach a 50% female Congress by the year 2050. Currently, only 24% of Congress is female, and the 50by2050 Project strives to bring us to full gender parity—a step in the right direction towards a representative body that accurately reflects the composition of our country.

Hundreds of college women have signed up with the 50by2050 Project to learn how they can start their political careers today. And we've interviewed and featured dozens of congresswomen and political leaders in *College Magazine* to show how they started their journeys while in college. A key element to the project is that I felt, and continue to feel, so inspired by is this image that unfolded before me with my eyes closed.

I couldn't have projected this without first taking the time to ask myself what moves me and to imagine that future in my mind. If you had simply asked me what future Amanda would be doing in her career without that visualization process, I probably would've said that I hope to be keynote speaking at universities—something I've already accomplished. I couldn't verbalize my ideal future until I took the time to fully envision it.

I want you to do the same thing—close your eyes and visualize your interests. Why exactly do I want you to do this? Because the act of visualization allows you to achieve the clarity that you may not have as you take in all the stimuli around you.

Most importantly, research shows you are more likely to achieve something if you first visualize it. Dr. Charles Garfield, the author of *Peak Performers*, has found in his research on top-performing athletes and other high achievers that peak performers are all visualizers. Before presentations, experienced speakers visualize a lecture hall jam-packed with 200 audience members. Before the championship game, peak athletes visualize annihilating their opponents. This tactic works in the career journey, too.

Before I sold enough ads to afford the cost of printing my first 5,000 copies of *College Magazine*, and long before I had even written the first article featuring my cover girl Rachel Wood, I visualized and designed a mockup in my notebook of what the magazine's cover would look like.

Before I won the University of Maryland's Cupid's Cup Business Competition created by founder and CEO of Under Armour, Kevin Plank, I visualized myself presenting and seeing the audience engage and nod in agreement as I spoke about how college students needed a guide to college. I imagined myself standing next to Kevin, holding that jumbo-sized check with $15,000 on the front.

Both of these visualizations came to fruition.

This is not magic; achieving the results of visualizations requires hard work. However, the visualization itself has the power to stimulate that work. It's important to envision your way from the first interview, to your first day on the job, to five years from now. So, let's get to it!

Here's what I would like you to ponder once your eyes are closed:

▷ What's an activity you can you do happily for hours on end and not even realize where the time went?

▷ What things do you enjoy most in life?

▷ What makes you laugh?

▷ What makes you light up inside?

▷ What gives you a feeling of pride?

Ready to visualize? Start by closing your eyes.

For all those skeptical readers out there eager to skip ahead, I highly recommend taking just one minute—a mere 60 seconds—to think about your passions.

If closing your eyes isn't working for you, then simply take some time for yourself. You could go on a walk, soak in your surroundings, and look for objects that spark your passion. Maybe it's your iPhone camera, the beautiful path in the woods, or that adorable dog running by with his owner.

The connection between your thoughts and the page is powerful. Let's make that happen by writing down your interests right now.

Step 2:
Glow up your strengths

Strengths are best realized through stories, but they're also best communicated through these stories.

My dad, Steven Nachman, was an admittedly mischievous kid. He always managed to get into trouble, and his teachers kicked him out of class as early as elementary school.

I remember hearing about the time when he hopped out of the classroom window to stomp on a pile of leaves that were on fire. At the time he assumed this act made him look like a hero—however, that was until the teacher discovered that he had been the one playing with the matches outside in the first place.

Later on, my dad went to Towson University and studied to be a history teacher; he had always enjoyed the subject and knew there were many teaching opportunities after graduation.

Being a teacher meant summers off, and during that time, my Dad would launch creative projects for fun. One year he wanted to start a snowball stand (or, for anyone not familiar with East Coast jargon, a snow cone stand). He called my mom, Caren, to bounce the idea off her. She was employed as a dental hygienist at the time—my mom recalls loving going to the dentist when she was a kid, and to say she's passionate about germ-free and cleanly living is an understatement.

My mom wasn't thrilled about the snowball stand idea, but she also wasn't surprised when she returned home that night to find a line of colorful bottles filled with snowball flavoring lined up on the kitchen counter. That was my dad. He had an idea and he made it happen.

In fact, the snowball stand was just one of his many ideas. Another year he brought home thin rubber material to cut and craft his own stamps to sell at a teacher's convention. At the following year's convention, he brought a stack of t-shirts to sell that he had gotten printed, blazoned with the saying "Teachers do it with class" on the front. The shirts practically flew off the shelf. He decided to take his success to the next level by inviting his friends and family to invest in a magazine ad for the t-shirts to see if he could drive more sales. He had quite a few takers after seeing how excited he was—everyone doubled their investment. His energy became contagious, generating interest and support from everyone around him.

The t-shirt success sparked another idea: Maybe he would start his own t-shirt printing company.

After finding a building to start his printing business, my dad ditched his teaching job and launched The T-Shirt Loft, which gave him the creative outlet he had always craved. Twenty years later, he merged with a friend's company to expand into the souvenir business and become United Souvenir and Apparel.

His journey took a substantial amount of work and demanded years of passion, determination, and creativity, but it ultimately ended in financial success. Just last year, my dad sold his business successfully and retired. #LikeABoss

My dad is a great example of identifying individual strengths—in his case, especially his creativity and perseverance—and leaning on those strengths to turn passion into a career. Don't get me wrong; that's not to say my dad woke up every single morning thrilled to sell, print, and ship t-shirt orders. Unfortunately, there will never be a job that's 100 percent all fun and no work. However, this business allowed him to flex his creativity, travel to gift tradeshows, work with my mom, who joined the business once it took off, and also work with my brother, who he later hired and who, to this day, is working with the new owner to take the business to the next level.

When you determine your strengths, you may not realize yet how they can align with your future career. My dad never would have anticipated that, as a history major on the path to teaching, he would go on to have a successful career in the apparel industry. But his story just goes to show that when you recognize and lean into your strengths, *and maybe use just a little mischievousness*, you can make magic happen.

Even if you spend hours practicing your hover board tricks in your free time for your YouTube channel, this shows that you are persistent and that you clearly have the creative skills—even if your only subscriber is your mom.

You probably didn't even realize that your ability to convince your Key Club to create a variety show as the fundraiser for the year was an example of your leadership strength. How about when you actually pulled the event off and students bought tickets to see the show? Did you research, plan, and execute? Why yes, yes you did. You go, Glen Coco.

Investigate your strengths by thinking about where you thrive. Do you thrive when you're in the spotlight, solving problems, communicating with others or planning events? Are you reliable? Are you innovative? Are you flexible?

Example Strengths

Ambitious	Great Communicator
Analytical	Mindful Planner
Authentic	Leader
Creative	Motivated
Dedicated	Team Oriented
Excellent Presenter	Time Management
Flexible	Skilled Writer

Christine DiDonato, founder of Career Revolution and Awesome-Boss.com, wanted to hire someone with planning skills and had an applicant who shared a story about planning her family reunion. In her interview the applicant broke down all the logistic details she needed to handle, explained how she created the reunion agenda, and even shared the way in which she determined which family members would room with whom (taking into consideration any family dramas, of course).

"That's a skill: conflict resolution," said Christine. "I thought—wow, that's a skill I could use. I could give this person anything, and she'll figure it out."

Perhaps you never thought to share your own life stories during a job interview but consider that these moments are the ones where your strengths shine. These life skills are transferable.

Even the most qualified and talented people need to take the time to identify their strengths. My editor in chief at *College Magazine* in 2015, Daniel Kuhn, held our internship position during his senior year at Penn State. He soared as one of my most talented editors and writers and helped grow our team by 50% through his leadership. I always saw Dan as a confident student with maturity well beyond his years. He wasn't modest either—he knew he was a skilled editor in chief.

But when Dan graduated, even he, the editor in chief who led 60 students and helped attract tens of thousands of daily readers to CollegeMagazine.com, fell off graduation's metaphorical cliff. Dan faced rejection from 20 job applications and felt lost in his career journey.

Dan was invited to interview at a few organizations but never received a job offer. After hearing this, he and I hopped on a call to practice his interview skills.

I asked him in a mock interview, "Tell me about your role as editor in chief at *College Magazine*." He said that he oversaw a team of student writers and editors and determined which articles would get published.

I was shook. He was able to sum up his entire year at *College Magazine* into one very dull sentence.

I pleaded to him, "Please tell me this is not how you describe your role and your strengths." The editor in chief role description alone is 10 times that length. If you describe your role in fewer words than the role description, there's something wrong with that picture.

After asking some very specific questions to poke at the details of Dan's role with *College Magazine*, Dan recognized that he was in fact leaving out an incredible amount of information. He was underselling himself, big time.

In that conversation, we reconstructed his brief overview into a true storytelling opportunity. Dan practiced answering that same question, but this time with a breakdown of his strengths.

Dan was a leader at *College Magazine*. He helped shape the team by co-leading interviews of prospective student writers. He taught dozens of our writers key writing strategies such as active voice, show vs. tell, and sentence structure variation. He trained new editors to help them become leaders. Not to mention, he reliably published eight articles a day on *College Magazine,* which collectively reached hundreds of thousands of readers.

Dan's top strengths that could be seen in his story are leadership, communication, and reliability.

ACTION:

Storytelling

Breaking down your strengths through storytelling sets you apart from the competition. "Be specific in an interview," said Sarah Bidnick, SVP of marketing at TodayTix. "When a candidate is a little too vague about why something might interest them... or what motivates them, it can be really difficult to differentiate them from the other candidates."

Nathan Young, founder of Greater Good Storytelling, helps individuals and organizations connect with their audience through the art of storytelling. "There is a very practical element of storytelling that is so key for job interviews," he said. "Being able to relate your experiences through the context of stories, that can really give the person interviewing you a sense of who you are and what you are capable of doing."

On Dan's next interview he did exactly that. First, he networked with another *College Magazine* graduate, who introduced him to the publication *TheStreet.* When he got the interview for the social media writer position, Dan shared his strengths through his story and ultimately conveyed his passion. Because of this, he got the gig!

What are your strengths? Let's not be shy here. This is your moment to brag. Write down 20 strengths right now.

Now connect three of these strengths to a concrete story (or all ten of them, if you can!). For example, if you wrote "reliable," "organized," "communicative," and "problem solver," then you might tell a story of that time you were asked by your friend to coordinate her wedding, even though you'd never done anything like it before. You said yes, and ultimately had to think on your feet on multiple occasions, including moving the whole ceremony inside to a new venue due to inclement weather. Her big day went off without a hitch, all thanks to you. (This is actually a true story about my friend Taylor.)

Now tell your story. Take to your journal and write down five stories where you've demonstrated your strengths.

Step 3:
Realize you've got values too

Values lie at the heart of the passion equation. (The equation isn't that complex; you can stop stress sweating.) Values are both the principles you live by and the causes you care about.

Don't skip past this part, thinking, *Values—that's only for people with strong religious convictions or serious do-gooders.* Nope, we all have values, whether we realize it or not.

Oftentimes our values hide within our internal code of conduct, passed down from our parents. Ever heard of the Golden Rule? This simple notion of reciprocity to treat others as you would like to be treated isn't just a nice saying—it's actually a value. See? Told you.

Example Common Values

Authenticity	Fun	Optimism
Adventure	Growth	Recognition
Balance	Honesty	Responsibility
Challenge	Influence	Stability
Community	Leadership	Teamwork
Creativity	Learning	Trustworthiness
Fairness	Meaningful Work	Wealth

As for the causes you care about, you don't have to be a saint to have community, national, or global issues on your radar. In fact, you can care about a cause and simply share information about it on social media or talk about it with your friends. Even changing your Facebook profile picture to show support for the latest movement helps to raise awareness.

These efforts, or simply talking about a cause, can have an impact ripple effect by bringing an issue to the forefront.

Perhaps after you spend a little time thinking and talking about what you care about, you even may decide to act. This could be in the form of volunteering, fundraising, donating, or getting involved in a relevant organization. Taking action on the causes you care about will, in turn, generate more passion for the cause. This energy will help you feel more connected to the cause than you ever thought possible.

When you identify your values, you can align them with places you want to work. You can even discover companies that you've never heard of by searching for ones that uphold your values.

If you value family time, vacation, flexibility, and work/life balance, you can find a company that also shares these principles. Maybe the company encourages its team to work from home part-time. Maybe another believes in unlimited vacation days for their employees—yes, that's a real thing! Check out Hubspot, Dropbox, and StichFix. Some companies even give their employees travel stipends. Take a look at Full Contact, Evernote, and Epic Systems. Sign me up.

Perhaps, like Sydney Foster, an editor at *College Magazine* and student at the University of Denver, you care about environmental protection. You may want to work for a company that focuses on sustainable practices, donates proceeds to rainforest preservation, or hosts a monthly beach cleanup.

Just because you value something doesn't mean it's the end-all-be-all in where you work, but it may be the additional element that helps connect you to your dream career. Your values can differentiate you. They can be the cherry on top of the strongest candidate sundae.

As for me, I live by a principle of integrity. I strive each day to demonstrate this to myself, my team, and everyone I work with through *College Magazine* and Find Your Passion Career. How do I do this? I'm so glad you asked. I have always envisioned creating a media empire with *College Magazine*, but in order to achieve this, I am not willing to compromise my integrity. For instance, there are shortcuts in the display-advertising world to trick consumers into viewing more ads. Instead, I stick to the best practice rules and focus on creating a positive experience for our readers. This is just one small example of how I am sticking to the person I want to be, rather than caving by doing whatever I can to achieve an arbitrary numerical goal.

I once spoke with a college student at one of my Find Your Passion Career events who shared with me and his class that he wanted to be a financial advisor. He explained that his primary goal was to make millions of dollars. Since we were on the topic of values, I asked him what he valued most. His response: nothing. He then added that he was willing to do anything necessary to make bank. *cue awkward silence* While I'm sure there are plenty of people who think similarly, I was surprised to hear this candid admission out loud.

At first, I wasn't even sure how to offer him career advice. But then I thought of my friend Douglas Boneparth, a Certified Financial Planner (CFP), financial advisor, and author of *The Millennial Money Fix*. He has been successful in his passion career by teaching his clients how to be financially responsible, advising on savings plans and how to choose the best possible investment approaches, all the while keeping in mind his clients' unique goals and lifestyles.

I explained to the student what it actually means to be a successful financial advisor; he would need to build trust with his clientele for them to feel comfortable having him handle their money, like Douglas with his thoughtful advising. And you can't build trust without first showing that you care.

Moving forward, this student will definitely need to reexamine his values if he wants to achieve his goals in a fulfilling way. Without values, even something as simple as caring for others' success, you will be hard-pressed to build meaningful connections and relationships that will help you advance in your career.

Chris Ducker, virtual CEO and speaker, offered this sage advice at the event Best Year Ever Blueprint: You must serve first and sell later.

Spend some time thinking about the principles you live by. How do you appear to the world? Do you value kindness, honesty, growth, individuality, leading by example, respect, or positivity? Look at the crowd you surround yourself with, your friends and family, and the people you admire most. What do they value? Their values might inspire you.

In your education and community service assignments growing up, you were taught to help and serve others—and that's because working together is essential for advancement in the real world. The real world may feel a little dog-eat-dog sometimes but ask anyone at the top how they got there; they'll be hard-pressed to take all the credit. No one achieves success without mentorships, meaningful relationships, and a helping hand.

You will not succeed alone. Prepare to look to your values to guide you on your career journey.

When you begin to reflect on what you value and the causes you care about, you might find there's truly an unlimited number to choose from. Think about things like education, the environment, politics, LGBTQ+ equality, women's rights, and health care. You can even search online and research hundreds of nonprofits and non-governmental organizations (NGOs) that dedicate themselves completely to a cause. Not to mention for-profit companies that support causes by donating money and time.

In other words, you can value education and work for an organization such as Room to Read, an international nonprofit that transforms the lives of millions of children in low-income communities by focusing on literacy and gender equality in education. Or you could work for a private company like Voxy, an English language-learning web and mobile platform, with the vision of teaching the world to speak English. These are just two examples of millions where you can connect your values to a career.

I'm passionate about education (hello, *College Magazine*) and equality for all. I support these causes by donating my personal time, volunteering each week with Reality Changers, a local San Diego program that helps disadvantaged high school students get accepted and graduate from college. I meet with a cohort of 25 students in City Heights, San Diego and assist the students in writing their college application essays. I also volunteer at events and fundraisers throughout the year with the Human Rights Campaign supporting equal rights and protections for the LGBTQ+ community.

Had you asked me in college about what I value, I probably would have said something like, "*Ronald McDonald House?*" At that point in my life I was totally clueless about my values and the causes I supported. Ronald McDonald House just happened to be my sorority's philanthropy.

In other words, I inevitably fell into that cause by default. I was living life unintentionally. You may feel similarly, and if you do, that's okay.

I didn't discover how important human rights were to me until I was invited to a Human Rights Campaign event in D.C. and felt moved by the speakers. I realized how much I cared for access to education for women after I read *Half the Sky: Turning Oppression into Opportunity for Women Worldwide* by Nicholas D. Kristof and Sheryl WuDunn. And I uncovered my passion for equal representation of women in government after the 2016 election, naturally. This inspired me to launch the 50by2050 Project.

It's 100 percent alright if you don't have any causes you care about today. It's never too late to start caring, and you can start right this second. If you begin thinking about it, you will be more open to discovering causes that resonate with you. And when you have a cause you feel passionately about, that's just another way to further differentiate yourself and align yourself with a career.

ACTION:

Connecting values to vocations

Either pull from your current values and causes or start fresh today. Then, write them down.

Now that you've identified your interests, strengths, and values, you can link them together to fully understand your passion—even if it's more than one. These three elements combine into a powerful force. And when you take the time to uncover them, connect them, and speak them, you are unstoppable!

Starting first with your values, search for five organizations that connect to one of your values and write them down.

4

CAREERS BEYOND THE BASIC

Now that you've successfully unlocked your passion, it's time to connect your interests, strengths, and values to a career. Most likely, this will be a nonlinear career. And even more likely, it will be a 99-percent career.

But what's a "nonlinear career" or a "99-percent career"? And how come no one has ever said these words to me before?

A nonlinear career is a job position that doesn't follow a direct path from a major or specialty, while a 99-percent career is a career that doesn't fall within the top 1 percent most recognizable brands.

For example, a career in marketing for a nonprofit like Camfed (the Campaign for Female Education) doesn't necessarily require a direct path. Camfed raises money to invest in girls and women in poor rural communities in sub-Saharan Africa, helping them attend school and find success. While, of course, there are experiences and skill sets you need to succeed working for Camfed, they're specifically looking for someone who is passionate about their mission.

There isn't a single college major that leads to a role at Camfed. Many types of majors, from sociology, to English, to international relations, to even computer engineering, can prepare you with the skill sets for this type of career. The real path lies in how you complement your major outside of the classroom. Organizations such as Camfed look to your experiences and activities that connect to their mission. In fact, there are endless unique paths that could lead to such a career, as long as you are passionate about educating disadvantaged girls in Africa!

To connect to a career like this, you must first display your passion. But how do you start? Begin by telling stories about your participation in clubs, organizations, and other movements or causes that have similar missions. Perhaps you traveled to Africa to visit with a rural school and now you donate regularly to fund their library. Let's say you work or volunteer for a nonprofit educating disadvantaged students in your city. Or maybe you participated in a documentary that showed how important it is to empower young women.

With some research on LinkedIn, I broke down the career paths of some of Camfed's team:

> The director at Camfed previously held the role of impact manager at Pencils for Promise, an organization that works across the globe to build schools and create programs around the goal of education for all. He had experience serving communities in Malawi, Ghana, Laos, India, Kenya, and Guatemala. He's able to show his commitment to a career of service with a focus on educational access through his work.

> The director of global partnerships received her Ph.D. in Neuroscience and then her MPH in Global Public Health. She previously worked as an independent advisor for Insight Action Global in which she conducted research for

international NGOs to make strategic recommendations for global health projects in developing economies.

▷ The senior donor relations manager at Camfed previously worked as a developmental associate at Inner-City Scholarship Fund. Before that, she was a first grade sheltered English immersion teacher at Boston Public Schools.

▷ The executive advisor previously founded DailyWorth, a leading financial media platform for women.

For just one organization, notice how varied these paths are!

You can do this too for any company you're researching. Simply look at LinkedIn to learn the career paths current employees have taken. When you look at the career trajectory of people who have the jobs you want, you can better understand a potential path for yourself.

Another example of a nonlinear career path is my dear friend and former editor in chief at *College Magazine*, Brian Cognato. He was an English and government and politics major at the University of Maryland. He loves to write, collaborate, and lead. He has a knack for uncovering the authentic, real stories of his subjects. He is also passionate about helping young people, which shined through in the volunteer work he did for years with 826DC, an organization that helps kids improve their creative writing skills.

Take a moment to consider his foundation:

PASSION	Journalism
INTERESTS	Sports, teamwork, writing
STRENGTHS	Driven, outgoing, compassionate
VALUES	Education, human rights
EXPERIENCES	*College Magazine*, 826DC, club basketball

Now what should Brian do with his career?

When I ask students this very same question during my live Find Your Passion Career events, the most popular answer is for Brian to become a newspaper reporter. I'll admit, that's not a bad idea, but that's an example of linear thinking. Point A to point B.

Oftentimes, linear opportunities mean more competition. Of course, Brian could have chosen to work in reporting, but he would have faced much stiffer competition in getting there and might have passed over opportunities that could have been a better fit for him. Endless opportunities exist in the world for someone like Brian who connects with his passion. If we are only thinking linearly, we limit ourselves.

So how can we get from point A to point *C?* And what did Brian actually end up doing?

Drumroll! After graduation, Brian went on to work for an organization called PeacePlayers International. He wanted to make an even greater impact in the world by working for a small organization where he could contribute directly to a mission while also learning the ins and outs of the nonprofit world.

You've probably never heard of PeacePlayers—and never would have if you didn't take the time to discover these nonlinear career opportunities. PeacePlayers is a nonprofit that uses the power of sport to unite, educate, and inspire young people to create a more peaceful world. Their programs connect kids from different backgrounds and oftentimes warring communities through the game of basketball.

Brian began his time with PeacePlayers as the development and communications associate (leveraging his passion, strengths, and values to get the job), in which he supported fundraising efforts and worked as the grant and report writer.

He then moved up the corporate ladder to serve as the technical assistance program director. Brian took the initiative to lead the entrepreneurial effort of growing Peace Players; he wrote a business plan, secured funding, and implemented projects in Tajikistan, Kyrgyzstan, Yemen, Ethiopia, Argentina, and Chicago, Illinois.

Imagine getting to make an impact like that. Brian's job was a lot of work, but it fit with his passions—and because he felt fulfilled in his job, all of his efforts made even more of an impact. Talk about living the dream.

In fact, the program lives on today even though Brian had moved on to a program operations specialist position at USAID (a 1-percent brand), and then moved on *again* to get his master's degree in Public Administration. Brian then served in a leadership position as the senior program officer for training and knowledge management at the Corporation for National and Community Service before moving on *again* to be an independent consultant for social sector organizations.

Although each of his roles have been very different, all these career pivots tie back to Brian's values. He's able to work on projects that are fulfilling and that have an impact far beyond himself—all because he followed his passion.

There's no exact written path to landing a job at a nonprofit like PeacePlayers. The key to getting a position there is in expressing passion for their mission and conveying your strengths in the skill sets they need to achieve their mission. You must actually care about their program and show it through your experiences and interests.

It sounds simple, but it all goes back to the passion exercises in Chapter 3. When you evaluate your passion, you know that you care strongly about something and then you can take that passion and connect it. You can't, and shouldn't, fake being passionate about a program like Peace Players (or any company for that matter).

Imagine if you disliked sports. It would be fairly challenging to connect with your co-workers at Peace Players. On the flipside, if you recall how playing basketball in high school helped you become a team player and feel more connected to your community and supported by your peers, then your passion is going to help you fit right in. Quit sleeping on your passion. Wake up and smell the opportunity.

Another example of a nonlinear path is Hilary Nachem Loewenstein. She's passionate about politics, communication, and women's rights. She was a government and politics major at the University of Maryland. Let's analyze what Hilary brings to the table.

PASSION	Politics
INTERESTS	Communications, public speaking
STRENGTHS	Decisive, passionate, persistent
VALUES	Women's rights
EXPERIENCES	Alpha Delta Pi sorority

What kind of career can Hilary seek?

I've heard several students suggest that Hilary should become a senator or congresswoman. Is that career competitive? Is it in the 1 percent? You bet. I'm not saying she couldn't be the next youngest member of congress, what I am saying is that there are so many opportunities to connect Hilary's passions beyond these few very coveted positions.

Hilary began her career journey on The Hill working as a staff assistant for the U.S. House of Representatives which gave her exposure to how government works and the role advocacy plays in impacting decisions.

Then she went on to work as a new media associate for Emily's List, a nonprofit that supports Democratic pro-choice female candidates on their journey to run for political office.

Hilary led the organization's online advertising program and helped design their list building campaigns. This was critical to the nonprofit's mission since Emily's List relies on its grassroots community of millions of supporters. Additionally, she wrote, compiled, and executed media buys (organizing and purchasing advertising campaigns based on the budget allotted) and worked with partners to help expand their subscribers. Imagine the experience Hilary was able to gain working for Emily's List.

From there Hilary brought her newly acquired skill sets to her role as the new media director for the Tammy Baldwin for Senate campaign. Imagine being passionate about politics and getting to be part of a campaign in which you successfully help your candidate become a senator—and not just any senator, but the first openly LGBTQ+ senator.

Hilary continued to work in politics including managing a statewide campaign and now works at Bully Pulpit Interactive helping run fully integrated marketing campaigns.

Brian and Hilary are examples of people who have pursued their passions within the first 10 years after college graduation. But what about someone who has been working for more than a decade in multiple nonlinear careers? Let's evaluate that scenario.

Julie Reisler has a multi-passionate career, which is evident in her diverse career journey. Today Julie is CEO of Empowered Living, a multi-time TEDx speaker, host of *The You-est You* Podcast, and the author of the *Get a PhD in You* series. She's passionate about helping you discover what sparks your fire for your life.

On her path to where she is today as an author and a life coach and speaker, Julie worked in both the nonprofit and corporate worlds. But even from the get-go her focus was always on her passion. Choosing her major at the University of Rochester, Julie knew that her education had to align with her passion for understanding how humans feel and express their emotions. She initially considered chasing this passion through the pre-med track. Instead, she double majored in psychology and public health, which she found to be the perfect combination for her passions and strengths.

After graduation she worked for Hillel International, a nonprofit organization focused on building Jewish communities on college campuses and engaging Jewish students. "One of the things I really started to get interested in was having a deeper spiritual connection to myself, to others," Julie said. She flourished in this environment.

One day, while she was working on running an international social justice program with Hillel, she visited a Panera Bread restaurant (only nine existed at the time) and was instantly drawn to the community she found there. Julie recalls having an "inner wisdom thought" that told her to apply to work with the company.

She submitted her resume and was offered a position as a manager. Julie eagerly accepted—and was told if she worked for five to six months learning operations, their corporate office would create a position for her. And they stayed true to their word. After six months, Julie was hired for the corporate team and went on to work with Panera Bread for 11 years as director of recruiting and guest relations. Her biggest take away from this experience is to trust your gut and make opportunities for yourself, even if you don't see one available.

"Opportunities are everywhere. This [Panera Bread job] didn't exist; this wasn't a position. I just trusted my intuition," Julie said.

While working with Panera Bread, Julie began to explore her other passions through continued education and side-hustles. She went back to school for her Master of Health and Wellness Coaching and Nutrition while still working full-time. She then created an intensive personal development program and led the program as the head coach.

While grinding on these side hustles, Julie had a "light bulb" moment that told her to chase her passions for coaching. "I wanted to do something where I was on fire about my purpose and passion," she said. She eventually left Panera Bread to follow her passion full-time.

"When we are listening and tuning and creating from that place of passion and purpose that's really where the magic happens," Julie said. Now an average day in her life changes on the reg but typically includes investing in herself by meditating, going to the gym, holding interviews for her podcast, speaking at events, and even traveling internationally to lead retreats for women.

For Julie, the thread of her career was following her heart, intuition, and interests every step of the way. She even created positions for herself and eventually brought her own coaching business into fruition.

Barbara Bry's journey is another example of a multi-passionate, nonlinear career path. In college, Barbara wasn't sure what she wanted to do but majored in sociology because she knew she needed to graduate in three years to save money.

Today, Barbara has achieved a successful career as a high tech-entrepreneur and is currently president pro tempore of the San Diego City Council representing District 1. She's even running for mayor of San Diego!

Barbara was raised by a single mom who always struggled to make an income comparable to her male peers. When Barbara's mother bought her first home, she had to have a male co-signer on her house because of the gender inequity at the time. Inspired by her mother, Barbara discovered a passion for equality for women.

Throughout her career, Barbara followed this passion, fighting for the advancement of women in the classroom and the workplace. After graduating from UPenn, she attended Harvard Business School during a time when women made up only 12% of the student body.

Barbara's personal experiences, as well as seeing her mother facing gender discrimination, fueled her to start Athena San Diego and Run Women Run, organizations which empower women to enter positions of leadership in the STEM and political fields. In the tech community, Barbara has been involved in the early stages of multiple local high-tech companies including ProFlowers.com. She's a great example of someone who chose to pursue something new (in her case, technology startups) even though she didn't go to school for it nor was technology her native language.

As an entrepreneur, she places a focus on ensuring that these jobs in tech fields are open to everyone in the community. Her passion to empower women has also influenced her professional career in politics.

Her experience working with Run Women Run and other political campaigns, as well as encouragement from her daughter, Rachel, ultimately inspired her to run for a seat of her own.

After winning the election for City Council as an underdog candidate in 2016, Barbara now works with a team to understand the needs and happenings of the community. She places an emphasis on teamwork—both during her campaign and now in her office as a councilwoman.

Barbara shares, "In everything I've done in life that's been successful, it's because we've been a team. You can't do anything like this by yourself." (Remember the importance of meaningful relationships in the "values" part of the passion equation?)

Barbara's typical day includes hosting team meetings to discuss important issues and legislation, meeting with the council, and attending community events to connect with her constituents face-to-face.

"I've been blessed that in my life I have followed my passion—almost every day that I've gone to work, I've really looked forward to being there," Barbara said. "I've been very blessed to be able to do that."

What's so fascinating about nonlinear career paths is there's often a thread connecting each set along the way that you can only see when you look back—just like Julie's thread connecting her experience with Hillel to her coaching business and Barbara's thread linking her interest in entrepreneurship to running for mayor. In fact, Barbara leans on her experience working in a tech startup when it comes to running a political campaign.

"I ran my campaign like a startup. As a startup, you never have enough money, you have to be scrappy, you have to do a little bit with a lot, and [with] us, it was having the hundreds of volunteers to help get our message about," Barbara said in our interview with her in *College Magazine*.

Don't worry so much right now about how the dots of your career will connect. They will eventually.

I couldn't always see the connection between my Troll doll apparel business as a kid, creating the Fraternity Men of Maryland calendar, or applying for the Quest honors program with starting *College Magazine*. But when I look back, it all makes sense to me. It all feels meant to be. Throughout the journey, obvi there were moments when I felt lost and unsure if I was on the "right path."

If you have that feeling, just know that you are not alone. As long as you're following your gut, your heart, and your passion, you will get there.

I without a doubt questioned if I was on the right path when I felt stuck in my first consulting job. But, in hindsight, although I hated the job, I still learned from that experience when I discovered that I crave creativity in my career. Similarly, I remember feeling overwhelmed that the Fraternity Men of Maryland calendar wasn't an overnight success. *cue eye roll* But that experience taught me the importance of testing a minimal viable product and communicating with an audience, both skill sets that I still use today.

There's no right or wrong path. There's the path you choose—and it will be most fulfilling if it's the one that aligns with your passion.

If these nonlinear career examples don't align with your passion career, that's okay! This is simply a reminder to look outside of the obvious career options that first come to mind. Next, we'll go over how a nonlinear career significantly increases your chances of getting a job at all, especially a job you like.

Ballerinas are cutthroat

A linear career is a direct path. For example, if you love dance and choreography, you major in dance and you become a choreographer, right? But did you know that becoming a choreographer is one of the most competitive jobs?

Top Competitive Careers[13]

1. Choreographers
2. Poets, lyricists, creative writers
3. Athletes and sports competitors
4. Sales agents, securities & commodities
5. Sound engineering technicians

Don't even get me started on the linear career of dance! According to backstage.com, only about 3 percent of dancers actually go pro.[14] But just because you may not be in that 3 percent, doesn't mean you can't take your passion, talents, and experience in the dance world and connect it to your future career. Remind me to never confront a ballerina in a dark ally, not only are they fit, they are used to stiff competition.

Why should you give up your love for dance just because you didn't make the 3 percent cut? It's a shame how many of us abandon our passions because it's too competitive and move on to something completely different—when at the very core our passions are what make us unique.

Picture that you were a dancer but didn't have the opportunity to go pro. Do you spend the next few years ugly crying watching Dance Moms and complaining about that girl's sloppy pirouette? No. What if you could continue to feel the sensation that you get from dance throughout your entire career? Goals, amirite? A simple Google search for "careers in dance" will present you with endless opportunities. Perhaps your love for dance could take the form of supporting the arts through education. Maybe you could work in arts administration or for a dance company. Dancers and dance companies need marketing—imagine building a website or creating the promotional materials for a dance company.

Let's say you're passionate about dance and science. You can link both to a career in dance medicine or physical therapy with a specialty in dancers. Dancers' success relies on these passionate individuals who help them recover from injuries. And you get to stay involved in the dance community.

Now that you understand some of the most competitive, linear careers, let's take a look at the careers that offer the most opportunities in today's economy. These are the fastest growing industries.

Top Opportunity Careers[15]

1. Wind turbine service technicians: 57% growth
2. Home health aid: 37% growth
3. Occupational therapy assistants: 33% growth
4. Information security analyst: 32% growth
5. Genetic counselors: 27% growth

There's no one single path to arrive at these "opportunity careers." In other words, they're nonlinear. But that's what makes the journey so exciting—it's a path that calls for passion. You have to uncover and find your own way there.

For instance, you could have a degree in the arts or business but, tied with passion and experience, you could become a statistician or translator, two additional emerging fields. I was an English major who worked as a government consultant after college because I was part of a program called Quest (a cross-collaborative honors program offered by University of Maryland) in which I worked on challenging consulting projects.

Just because you didn't major in a language doesn't mean you can't use the fact that you are bilingual and passionate about communication and bringing together diverse communities to become a professional translator. ¡*Vámonos!*

The fact that some of the fastest growing jobs are nonlinear makes a pretty clear case for embracing this path. While discovering a nonlinear career may seem daunting, you *can* make it happen. And I'm here to help. There are a lot of ways to research and discover these opportunities.

Creeping on your career

Now that you understand the opportunity, you need to actually find these careers. It's likely that you are not familiar with many of these career paths. But they're not that tricky to uncover, I promise.

How do you explore the unknown? The first step is super straightforward: Lean on your homeboy Google.

For example, let's say you're most passionate about animals. In a search for "animal organizations," I discovered dozens of nonprofit organizations that support animals—but I also found an interesting article on *The Muse* titled "7 Companies That Are Perfect for Animal Lovers."

The list featured Rover, a company that connects pet owners to caregivers, and when I was researching for this book, they had positions available for a copywriter, a partnership specialist, a senior data engineer, an IT support specialist, and a customer experience representative, just to name a few. Imagine connecting your diverse strengths and skill sets to a career that embraces your passion for animals. And if you're going to work for a company like Rover, you are much more likely to succeed and feel fulfilled if the company's mission aligns with yours.

You can even break this process down further. Select one of your interests, strengths, or values. Now search for career opportunities that connect directly. For an interest like music, search for companies for music fanatics or organizations that support musical arts. For a strength like leadership, search for companies that teach leadership development. For a value like continued learning, search for companies that offer exceptional continued learning programs. This exercise will help you expand your career opportunity list even more.

Even if you spend just 30 minutes a day researching companies you haven't heard of, you're opening yourself up to new opportunities.

Pro Tip:

Idk about you, but for me, Googling and just bookmarking the companies that I find interesting is a recipe for forgetting. Instead, actively keep track of your research. Start by writing down a couple companies you discovered through your search. Dare I say, open up Google sheets too?

Once you find a company that sparks your interest, prepare to read and learn. If you only spend a couple of minutes on the company's website, you aren't giving yourself ample time to get a full understanding of the mission, vibe, and company culture.

Be intentional with your research. Start with the company's "About Us" page or their mission statement. Then dive into their blogs. Many companies will blog about their capabilities or accomplishments or simply share industry news. You can get an idea of what this company stands for by reading the content they produce.

Follow the company on social media to get a sense of what they care about. Treat your prospective company like a first date—get curious! Ask yourself meaningful questions to uncover the company's intentions and your potential fit. Remember, just like dating, it takes two to tango, so does employment. You want your date to be a good candidate for you just as much as you want to be a good candidate for them. Ask yourself:

- ▶ What are the company's goals?
- ▶ How is the company successful?
- ▶ How does my passion connect with the organization?
- ▶ What are the ways I can contribute to the company's vision?

Keep in mind that the internet doesn't always tell the truth. Much like that guy you knew in high school who only posts selfies at extravagant parties or kicked back at the beach, organizations often broadcast idealized images of themselves that they want the public to see.

It's important to consider other perspectives. One way to do this is to seek out articles written *about* the company. Look for news pieces on the company versus press, which is often based on press releases sent by the company. Depending on the type of company, you may search for product launch news, accomplishment coverage, event reviews, interviews with the CEO, and more.

Dig even deeper by reading the employee reviews (plus transparent salary information!) on GlassDoor.com. The best way to get a real feel for the company is to talk to those who work there. Just like I did with Camfed, start looking for real employees of the company so you can get an idea of their career journeys.

With this research, you'll feel prepped to reach out to employees directly. Don't worry about this just yet; I'll break down how to do that in Chapter 7, stay tuned.

At the moment it's time to see if the company is actively looking for someone like you. Browse for job opportunities or open positions on the company's career website. This will also help you see which areas of the company are growing the fastest.

Even if the only open positions you see online are for web developers or senior managers, don't fear. Remember the stat on job postings. You never know until you ask; you'd be surprised how many companies are hiring and looking for you but haven't had the time to create a posting. Just because you don't see a position that seems like a good fit for you, doesn't mean you shouldn't connect with the organization.

Don't you want your career journey to be plentiful with opportunity? Duh!

ACTION:

Mark your research time on your calendar today to get started.

5

INSTANT GRATIFICATION
IS *SO* LAST SEASON

Everything leading up to this point has been reflection and research. You looked internally and homed in on your interests, strengths, and values. Then you looked externally for nonlinear and the 99-percent careers that you didn't know were out there.

Now it's time to take your research and synthesize it into your personal career vision statement.

According to Stephen Covey, author of *The 7 Habits of Highly Effective People,* "All things are created twice; first mentally; then physically. The key to creativity is to begin with the end in mind, with a vision and a blueprint of the desired result."

Vision allows you to think long-term instead of focusing on what you want in the immediate short term. What do you want five to ten years from now, versus what you want this year?

When we're not thinking with an end goal in mind, we're often thinking reactively. We focus on what we *don't* want in our lives versus what we are striving to achieve. (Law of Attraction PEOPLE.) But when you think with the end goal in mind, you can strive for greatness in your future career choices. Keeping the end in sight will mobilize you the way vision can mobilize a movement.

Vision is key to movements. Beginning in 2005, the Human Rights Campaign (HRC) advocacy group had a vision for marriage equality. Around then, HRC launched their Religion and Faith Program to engage clergy to advocate for LGBTQ+ people. This helped create the DC Clergy United for Marriage Equality, which contributed to the legalization of same-sex marriage in the District of Columbia in 2010.[16]

HRC's efforts, such as raising and contributing $20 million to re-elect President Obama as well as supporting marriage-related ballot measures, all tied back to their vision of equality for all. It wasn't until 2015, when *Obergefell v. Hodges* went to the Supreme Court and legalized same-sex marriage across the nation. That's a 10-year journey! And it all started with a vision.

Keep in mind, marriage equality wasn't achieved by HRC alone; dozens of grassroots organizations fighting for LBGTQ equality are to thank for this incredible vision realized. But identifying and declaring a vision just like HRC is the first step in the right direction to achieving success.

Born in 1985 in Baltimore, Maryland, growing up I couldn't imagine a future where same-sex couples could marry. I lived many years closeted and afraid of revealing my true self. Today I'm able to live a fulfilling, authentic life as an openly out woman because of visions like these coming to fruition.

There's still more progress to be made in fighting for LGBTQ+ equality, and I actively volunteer and support the mission. I firmly believe that our continued progress stems from vision.

Vision will change your life and impact others as well. Imagine your vision as a stone thrown into the water. As your vision hits the water and you embark on your journey, ripples flow, impacting everyone and everything around you.

The Human Rights Campaign's vision changed my life. My vision for *College Magazine* changed my life. And all for the better. Are you ready to change *your* life for the better and achieve your passion career?

Cue bracelet snap

A vision is just a fancy word for a BIG future goal. While goal setting typically happens at the beginning of a journey, I didn't begin this book asking you to create your vision on purpose—because first, we needed to address your mindset.

Take it from JJ Virgin, celebrity nutrition and fitness expert and four-time *New York Times* bestselling author, who connects her ability to set large visions directly with her power to influence her mindset.

When JJ began her career as a personal trainer, she was inspired by her mentor to wear a rubber bracelet and snap it every time she had a self-limiting thought. After enough snaps and a sore wrist, she realized how much we tend to doubt ourselves.

JJ explained that once you break the vicious cycle of these doubting thoughts, all you see is possibility. The bracelet exercise was just the beginning for JJ on her journey to building her personal brand and achieving big visions—starting with *How do I start earning enough to not have to get another job?* to *How do I impact one million people?* to *How do I help one billion people get healthy?*

After using that bracelet to train herself to see and eliminate self-doubt, JJ Virgin now sees only possibility. And because of this renewed confidence, she is always innovating and refining her vision.

Hopefully by now, we solved the problem of your "blank slate" mindset and identified your passion, which lies at the very heart of your vision statement. A strong, purposeful, and sustainable vision is completely grounded in your passion.

You may be thinking vision is something that companies have, not people. Or maybe you're already familiar with personal branding and understand that people can have visions, too—if so, awesome! Either way, you'll soon learn that vision is your compass, and just like it helps businesses and their employees navigate their journeys, you need one too.

No, I'm not saying that setting a vision for your life now will create a shortcut to the end result, nor will stating your vision make the road any less bumpy. However, as you move toward your vision, you'll be taking an intentional journey rather than an aimless one. And an intentional path will feel a lot smoother than the aimless journey.

Your vision, like your passion, can transform over time—but nevertheless, it's very important to set one and write it down ASAP.

"When you keep the vision in your head, it stays in your head," said Kristin Hayden, chief partnership officer for Ignite National, the movement to inspire young women to run for political office. "One of the ways to start manifesting what it is you want, one of the very first steps, is to actually write it down. It makes it concrete, you can see it, touch it."

My own career vision began in 2007 with the intention to create a national print magazine. I wrote this vision down in my very first business plan that I pitched to the Dingman Center for Entrepreneurship at the University of Maryland. Then, in 2009, my vision shifted to creating a national online magazine reaching half a million monthly readers.

By 2012, I set my sights higher with a vision to launch a media company with national advertising partners reaching a million monthly readers. Now, 10 years later, my vision is to grow my media company to include 75 campus chapters, reach 10 million monthly readers, and to be a keynote speaker at 100 campuses nationwide, helping millions of college students achieve their passion careers.

The average person will scoff at a vision this big. It sounds almost insane, right? But do you think Oprah Winfrey, Richard Branson, or Bill Gates would laugh at a vision like this? Not a chance. I'm not saying you need to strive to have a 1-percent success story like theirs—but if you want to get even close to having a job that's fulfilling, you better start dreaming, and dream big.

Dr. Sean Stephenson, a therapist, motivational speaker, and author of the international bestselling book, *Get Off Your "But,"* exemplified dreaming big. Despite being diagnosed at birth with a rare bone disorder that ultimately stunted his growth and caused his bones to be extremely fragile, Sean beat his survival odds. He lived until the age of 40, and I feel lucky to have seen him speak about success. He rolled up like a boss in his wheelchair to give his keynote talk at the Best Year Ever Blueprint event in 2019 with a simple yet powerful message: "You know there's something bigger for you. You are playing small. PLAY BIG."

He encouraged us all to set visions that excite and empower us. According to Sean, some great questions to ask yourself as you determine your vision are:

- ▸ Where are you going?
- ▸ What do you want?
- ▸ Who do you want to become?

Because I have set a big vision for myself, every day I feel fulfilled. I know I'm working toward an end goal. Each month, I look forward to my team meetings with my student editors and team members in which we celebrate our accomplishments and set an action plan to continue the momentum toward the vision. I enjoy helping thousands of students feel more confident and prepared for college through

College Magazine and I know that I am one step closer every day I work on editorial systems, writer training programs, teambuilding, and fully-integrated marketing campaigns.

When Kelly Livingston, a former *College Magazine* writer, reached out to tell me about her new job as a morning news anchor at Inland Northwest Broadcasting and to share how our writer-training program at *College Magazine* helped her to become a professional journalist, I confirmed the need for my vision.

Every time I launch a podcast filled with actionable steps for listeners to achieve their passion career, I can literally feel my vision materializing.

Reading the feedback from audiences who have attended my keynotes or workshops further validates the impact of my message. For example, reading this reaction from one student made all the hard work worth it: "You inspired me to take action and follow my dreams. After this, I will definitely take small steps to make my vision happen." *brb crying*

You've pushed aside self-doubt and discovered your passions—it's time for you to set a vision for the career you desire. Get ready for a career that makes you eager to wake up in the morning, and a career you are passionate about.

Bracelet: 0   You: 1

Vision is the new statement piece

By setting a vision, you'll be able to seek out opportunities that can help you get to where you want to be in your fulfilling career.

Laurence, now a line producer's assistant on the Netflix Original *You*, always dreamt of becoming a producer, but it wasn't until graduate school when he was assigned to jot down his vision, that he decided on a future creating feature films for a living. Soon after this assignment, he attended a networking event; his ears immediately perked up when he met a director who was in need of an intern for his independent film. He jumped on the opportunity. *Coincidence? I think not.*

Today, Laurence continues on his career journey and, with a distinct vision in mind and solidified in writing, he's able to follow a much clearer path that aligns with his passion.

Martin (Marty) Ringlein is a prime example of a visionary for his career; he's an incredibly successful serial entrepreneur and investor. Marty was also a presidential innovation fellow for the Obama administration working directly within the Executive Office of the President.

Prior to that, Marty launched "nclud," a research and design agency, which was acquired by Twitter in 2012.

His most recent startup, called "nvite," was acquired by Eventbrite in 2016. Today Marty works on future-proofing innovations for the company. He's on the lookout for the future technologies or industry shifts that could possibly put Eventbrite out of business (think the Netflix to Blockbuster) and helps the company stay ahead of the curve with new ideas.

His vision couldn't have foreseen these exact companies acquiring his startups—in fact, Twitter didn't even exist when Marty was in college—but do you think Marty could have reached such heights without a vision? Not a chance.

Marty set a vision for each step of his career and every project he began, starting with his University of Maryland Greek Yearbook side hustle in college, where he solved a problem by transforming the print project into an online experience. Every step of the way in his career journey, Marty has set larger-than-life visions to create inventive solutions to problems. It's his vision and his passion for that vision, which has driven others to believe in him, support him, and join him in achieving greatness.

Because your vision is inherently massive and lives in the future—it's not going to be perfect. A vision can be a messy stretch of an idea. It can be radical. It can be crazy. Dream big.

When it comes to achieving our visions, the road will unavoidably zigzag. You'll quickly learn to pivot along the way. For Marty, in his quest to finding the projects that clicked and worked, he tested plenty of ideas and minimal viable products (also known as MVPs, which are test versions of concepts used to gain feedback), and many of them didn't pan out. According to Marty, "This idea that we have to be perfectionists…often holds us back."

If you're a perfectionist like me, you have to learn to accept that your road to achieving is often undefined. You must accept that to achieve your vision, there will be surprises.

I'm talking about the kind of surprises like having to hand-distribute 40,000 magazines, getting rejected from three magazine editorial internships, or hearing "no" from dozens of advertisers until you finally hear that one "yes" that keeps you in business. (And yes, I personally encountered all these "surprises" while on my journey to achieving a six-figure business.)

But that's the great part about a vision: It's not judging you on your journey and it's also not set in stone.

"You don't have to achieve all of your goals or meet 100 percent of your passion every day the first few years of your career," said Christine DiDonato, founder of CareerRevolution. "It's really unrealistic. Be forgiving of yourself and say, 'I'm not alone—most people working are feeling the same stress I am.'"

Without a vision, you're simply playing small, going after easily achieved goals, or stumbling through life aimlessly. Now that you've unlocked your passion, don't waste another minute sitting idle while you hope to achieve something great.

According to therapist Dr. Sean Stephenson in his keynote, it's more important to have a goal than to achieve that goal. The goal itself keeps you in the direction you want, whereas achievements live in the past.

This is why I use the word "journey" so much when I speak about passion careers. It's not about where you'll end up; it's about the experiences along the way.

Go BIG or go home

Imagine that your intentional career, heading towards your vision, begins to unfold. That what you've dreamt about actually starts to manifest. This is only possible if you first set your vision, but what happens when you actually take action towards your vision? What does that look and feel like?

I spoke with Ben Simon, CEO of Imperfect Produce. He's working in his passion career, and his journey began with a single vision.

Ben didn't know what his career would look like early on, but he held hope for the world around him—starting with eliminating food waste on his campus at the University of Maryland. And that first idea paved the way for his career today at Imperfect Produce.

"I just wasn't that good of a student; I didn't enjoy it that much," Ben said of his time in college, "but [I found] this passion outside of school."

Ben felt determined to change his university's cafeteria policy around leftover food. If he could just get through the school's red tape, he could send the leftovers to a soup kitchen nearby. With this vision in mind, Ben took action.

After meeting with university administrators and making his case, he received approval. At just 21 years old, Ben manifested his first vision along with a team of classmates. He still remembers the reactions from the cafeteria chefs. "Going into the dining hall and partnering with the chefs; they're lit up with excitement... They feel good... They're helping the community," he said. The university chefs had always thought that their excess food would end up in the trash. Now they could see their leftovers could go to a better cause at a soup kitchen.

And when Ben and his team of student volunteers drove the first delivery of aluminum trays filled with freshly cooked meals to the neighborhood soup kitchen, he said it was a moment he would never forget. "You can see the recipients of the food light up as well. They're all smiles."

He created a successful process on his campus to reduce food waste, and from there Ben expanded his vision to create Food Recovery Network (FRN), a national nonprofit organization and movement.

"The vision for Food Recovery Network was, let's replicate this, let's scale this up to other colleges across the country. The phrase [we used] was 'we want to go national.'"

Ben and his team built a model that was used at one school, then two, then four, then thirteen, then twenty-one. Imagine seeing that kind of growth unfold.

FRN's vision grew along with their success, now redefined with a desire to expand to 500 and then 1,000 schools. "We want to make colleges the first industry where recovering food instead of wasting it is actually the norm," he said. "We're fulfilling that vision; we're at 230 colleges now."

After college, Ben continued to follow his passion in reducing food waste. During his time running FRN, Ben learned that 20 billion pounds of fruits and veggies go to waste on farms every year in the U.S., oftentimes because they don't live up to the cosmetic standards of grocery stores.

Ben and his colleague at FRN, Ben Chesler, decided to embrace and sell this "ugly" produce, and in 2015, Imperfect Produce was born.

When he started the company, he remembered his family's reaction: "They were like: 'That's never going to work out; people aren't going to pay for ugly fruit and vegetables.'"They felt his 30% discount wouldn't be nearly enough to attract customers used to the perfect fruits and veggies of large grocery chains.

But Ben stuck with his gut and turned his vision into a reality. Today he leads a team of over one hundred employees at Imperfect Produce. "I have a lot of fun at work; every day is different."

"When I started, I never thought that it would someday be a job for me, much less a whole company," he said. "It's been a pretty amazing journey."

Ben's success all began with his passion for wanting to help others and a vision for reducing food waste, which helped him create a road map and stay the course.

Kristin Hayden's passion career path also beautifully ties back to her ability to generate a larger-than-life vision and courageously go after these visions. Today, she is a high-energy, sought-after speaker on living your vision. She has spent her career creating opportunities for leadership, empowerment, and greater global engagement among historically underprivileged groups. She is an Ashoka Fellow, one of the world's leading social entrepreneurs, and the official spokesperson for the Global Access Pipeline, a collaborative network of organizations forming a pipeline for underrepresented groups in the U.S. preparing them for leadership in international affairs. And if that wasn't enough, she is also the chief partnership officer for Ignite in San Francisco.

When she first entered the workforce, Kristin knew she wanted to change the world and make an impact in the lives of young people.

Her passion career journey began in 2002. She felt inspired by her own language studies and travels abroad growing up and wanted to help low-income students gain access to similar life-changing experiences. With that passion driving her, Kristin founded the nonprofit, OneWorld Now! (OWN). OWN offers one of the only programs in the nation that spends at least one year preparing youth for study abroad, setting students up for success by providing leadership training and language lessons in Arabic, Chinese, and Korean, three strategically important languages that are not typically offered in American public schools. The organization focuses on providing access to study abroad opportunities to mostly low-income youth and students of color.

"[I wanted] to give more global opportunities particularly to underserved youth. All Americans need more of a global perspective in our education system, but I also see the disparities," Kristin said. "I wanted to level the playing field."

Just like Marty's minimal viable product (MVP), Kristin launched a pilot program at Ingraham High School in north Seattle with just 12 students. "I had no idea what I was doing. I had no experience starting a nonprofit organization. I had a vision, but that was it," said Kristin.

After a funding opportunity for kicking off the pilot program fell through, Kristin felt pressure to give in and explore a steadier career. Despite this pressure and being extremely disappointed at the time, she kept to her vision. "It's a good sign if people say that [your idea] is crazy or impossible—then you know you are probably onto something," she said. "I think that's the start of all visions, to actually be very bold about the change you want to see in the world and what it is you want to do."

Since then, OWN has expanded to include students from every high school in the Seattle Public School District, working with over 150 students each year—and the Jack Kent Cooke Foundation even deemed OWN one of the most innovative after-school programs in the U.S.

The results speak for themselves. In the 15 years since launching, OWN has served 1,500 youth directly in its yearlong immersion program while engaging over 3,000 youth through various elements of its programming. Over 98 percent of program graduates have enrolled in college, most being first-generation college students. OWN alumni have received scholarships and appointments with places like the Gilman Program, Rangel Fellowship, Fulbright, the U.S. Department of State, and more. Overall, OWN has leveraged nearly $2 million in scholarship funding to support low-income students to study abroad.

Talk about an incredibly impactful legacy that all began with a vision.

Once you've set your vision, Kristin encourages you to be open and to allow yourself to be pleasantly surprised by the journey, rather than being so attached to how you're going to get there. Think of anything bold you've done in your life and how you got there; the answer isn't usually "according to a perfectly outlined plan."

How do you write a vision? Think about your passion and what you want to achieve. Describe it. How do your interests, strengths, and values all come together to this one point with this vision for your future? I can't write your vision for you. Only you can determine your vision.

Here are a few vision statements from inspiring visionaries to help you form your own, courtesy of Stephanie Vozza at Fast Company:[17]

> ▷ Amanda Steinberg, founder of DailyWorth: "To use my gifts of intelligence, charisma, and serial optimism to cultivate the self-worth and net-worth of women around the world."

> ▷ Oprah Winfrey, founder of OWN, the Oprah Winfrey Network: "To be a teacher. And to be known for inspiring my students to be more than they thought they could be."

> ▷ Sir Richard Branson, founder of The Virgin Group: "To have fun in [my] journey through life and learn from [my] mistakes."

Consider what you would like to achieve in your career in the next three to five years, connecting your interests, strengths, and values. THINK BIG! The opportunities for your vision are endless.

ACTION:

Write your vision today and revisit it as often as possible.

6

DUE DILIGENCE: *THAT'S HOT*

You've set your vision and are bursting at the seams to get your show on the road.

First and foremost, give yourself a high five because determining your vision—the accumulation of your passions in a future plan—is one of the hardest parts to tackle. Now you're ready to start on your journey by taking action and creating intentional experiences. And most importantly, by being bold. So, let's do this!

What kind of actions should you take? Consider joining organizations, volunteering, interning, side hustling, and building up your experience in a way that connects directly to what you love. Choosing exactly where you spend your time is the next level of reframing your mindset, which we conquered at the start of this book: Are you sleepwalking your way through life, or are you adopting measures to live intentionally?

While you should strive to spend your time doing things that ignite your passion, you don't have to bail on your favorite improv team just because you don't want to pursue comedy as part of your passion career.

Focusing intentionally on your activities doesn't mean you can't still enjoy your current hobbies. Yes, you can be part of the running group in your neighborhood or take cooking classes even if they have nothing to do with your future vision for your career.

Just be sure to acknowledge that these are *hobbies*. Hobbies are great for blowing off steam and finding the pleasures in life. While they can be great for networking, they are less intentional in the sense that the people you meet through hobbies may not be connected to your passion career.

For the purpose of helping you achieve your passion career, we want to stay focused on intentional experiences that go *beyond* hobbies. When I say intentional experiences, I mean moments of dedicated time toward specific activities that connect directly to your career.

Major Key Alert: Prioritize your passion.

It took me a minute to fully learn this lesson. When I arrived at college, I was shooketh by the sheer number of student organizations I could join. The student activities fair was jam packed with opportunities, and I went cray, joining the Alpha Delta Pi sorority, the Quality Enhancement Systems and Teams (Quest) business honors program, club field hockey, the guitar club, and a handful of other totally random organizations. I was even a TA for my favorite Italian professor. I was so overwhelmed that I ended up having to drop a lot of these activities by the end of freshman year when I realized I wasn't Superwoman, and that there were less hours in the day than I thought when signing up.

Sometimes overachievers and hobbyists go to an event like a student activities fair and join just about everything that sounds fun. Rock climbing? *Yes, please!* Yoga club? *Namaste.*

This is a great way to learn more about what you like and dislike, but you're bound to overextend yourself—and once you've determined your passion, it's time to make *that* your priority.

For me, clubs were the perfect way to make new friends. I appreciated being involved in the campus community. But I also wasn't sure what I was most passionate about. As a matter of fact, I had never taken the time to ask myself what my passions or my career goals were—I just didn't know and blindly accepted that I didn't know. If I could go back in time, I would tell my freshman self to get a clue and join the school newspaper or magazine, but at the time I was just winging it. (And that's totally okay! The college experience, especially that first year, is largely about experimenting and figuring things out.)

Luckily by junior year I felt more connected to my interests and strengths—writing and editing—and I decided to test the waters with an internship. Everyone else seemed to be getting one, so that meant I should get one, too. *Right?*

I applied for three potential summer editorial internships at *Baltimore* magazine, *Washingtonian* magazine, and *Better Homes & Gardens* magazine. I even received an in-person interview for *Baltimore* magazine. I felt completely qualified: I loved writing, I had a strong GPA above 3.8, and… well, I guess that was where my resume ended. But I felt totally confident that I would land something.

Clearly, it wasn't enough, because I was rejected from all three internships.

After that last rejection came in, I was crushed. Maybe I wasn't qualified after all, and maybe journalism wasn't the right path for me.

If you've been reading closely, you should recognize the blank-slate mindset talking. Yes, I experienced it, too, and know it all too well.

Serendipitously, around the same time one of my professors assigned an informational interview project. We were tasked with connecting with a person in a career path that we admired. *Ah-ha!* I thought. *I'll reach out to the internship coordinator at* Washingtonian *magazine, and then once she meets me, she'll see that I was qualified all along.*

After one quick email to the internship coordinator, she agreed to meet me for an informational interview over coffee to learn more about her role. We met at a coffee shop in Washington, D.C. I remember getting dressed in my best (read: *only*) business professional outfit and feeling nauseous about navigating the 30-minute drive into the city from the University of Maryland.

My thoughts swirled; *Where will I find parking? What will it be like to meet one-on-one with a real-world professional? Am I wearing the right outfit?!*

Putting my fears aside, I felt confident in the fact that I had a list of questions fully prepared about how she landed a job at *Washingtonian* magazine and what her day-to-day looked like. Of course, my underlying motive was to impress her and make her realize that I was the perfect candidate for her internship—but at the very least, I would be able to show her that I could hold a pleasant conversation.

After I found a parking space close enough that I wouldn't have sweat stains when I arrived but far enough away that she wouldn't see me nervously fumble out of my car from the window of the coffee shop, we started our informal interview. At first, it went off without a hitch—until she explained that she began her editorial journey by getting involved in her university's magazine and newspaper. She said these clubs gave her the opportunity to get published and build her portfolio. Then, once she had real samples to her name, she applied for editorial internships.

Wait, what? I was supposed to have actual writing samples of my magazine writing abilities already? Eeeek.

This blew my mind. I hadn't given any thought to building a portfolio at that point in my career journey. I had never even considered writing for my campus magazine.

After the informational interview, I looked online and discovered that there were more than 10 publications on my very own campus.

I immediately emailed the editor in chief of the University of Maryland's lifestyle magazine, *Unwind.*

I hit the ground running, attending the very next on-campus meeting. I got to experience an article brainstorm process unfold. Then I watched as the editors in charge pitched concepts and writers selected the article topics that interested them most. I signed up to write a Ben Folds concert review. *Sham on!*

This was my opportunity to flex my writing skills, cover campus events, and get published in a real printed publication. I learned how to interview students about the latest spring sandals trends, cover live shows, and improve my writing through their editorial system.

In just three short weeks, there it was: my byline in physical print. *brushes off shoulder* I cut out the article and added it to a new folder tucked among my textbooks that I titled "Portfolio." I also saved the online PDFs, naturally.

I then submitted my polished published clips for my next editorial internship application at *Washington Spaces* magazine, a home and design publication and subsidiary of *The Washington Post.* I was told about the opportunity from a fellow English major who held the position the previous semester. And with my professional portfolio and networking skills working in tandem, I got the gig.

You can't control the rejection—and everyone will get rejected—but what you can control is feeling qualified. Therefore, the more time you invest in your passion, the more you build upon your strengths and experiences in that area, that will give your resume more clout and gives *you* more ways to demonstrate your strengths. With greater experience comes greater confidence. This scenario is the perfect recipe for scoring your passion career.

Here's just a snapshot of the organizations you can join while in college and after:

College: Choral Groups, Concert Band, Dance, Drama/Theater, Film Society, Fraternities, International Student Organization, Jazz Band, Literary Magazine, Marching Band, Model United Nations, Music Ensembles, Musical Theater, Opera, Pep Band, Radio Station, Sororities, Sports, Student Government, Student Newspaper, Symphony Orchestra, Television Station, and Yearbook

Post-College: Local Theatre, Improv, Girls in Tech, Young Entrepreneurs Council, Rotary Club International, and League of Women Voters

I searched on Meetup.com in San Diego, for example, and found a diverse number of organizations to join to help build your networking community and skill set: Exceptional Entrepreneurs, Business Networking, StartupSD, Young Professionals Network, San Diego, Online Advertising, Natural Hair and Wellness Meetup, Indie Creatives, San Diego Improv, 3D Printing, Sci-Fi Filmmakers, Women Who Code, and CyberTech San Diego iOS Developers.

Not only that, there are national professional organizations with local chapters you can join in college and after to further your experiences:

Public Relations Student Society of America (PRSSA): This student organization, with more than 300 chapters on college campuses, works with the Public Relations Society of America (PRSA) to advance the PR profession. They offer networking events, competitions, scholarships, and leadership opportunities for students (and professionals!) passionate about PR.

Phi Alpha Delta (PAD): PAD is a co-ed law fraternity, with 650 chapters nationwide, that focuses on professional advancement and community building for law and pre-law students. They even host one of the largest Mock Trial Competitions in the nation for law students.

The Society of Professional Journalists (SPJ): As a national organization with 250 chapters, SPJ helps students and journalists network and gain access to key training opportunities.

American Marketing Association (AMA): AMA is one of the largest marketing associations in the world. It aims to elevate the role of marketing and connect marketers with the resources they need for success.

Phi Delta Epsilon (PhiDE): The PhiDE fraternity student chapter is for students interested in the medical field to develop their leadership skills and connect with medical professionals.

American Society of Civil Engineers (ASCE): ASCE is the oldest engineering society in the country with the goal of advancing the profession through conferences and continuing education.

Zeta Phi Eta: Zeta Phi Eta is a campus fraternity that engages students in the communication arts and sciences.

ACTION:

What organizations align with your passion? What steps can you take next to join or get involved? Write it down!

Once you've taken the step to get involved, ask yourself:

▶ Is there more you can do to prioritize your passion?

▶ Can you attend more events for your organization?

> ▶ Can you connect with professionals who were once in
> your organization?

> ▶ Can you take on a leadership role—chapter president,
> club treasurer, social media manager, etc.?

Your answer to these questions should be a resounding "yes!"
Leadership roles within an organization will take your commitment to your passion to the next level. I'll cover how you can build upon your skill sets through leadership in Chapter 10, but first things first, let's talk internships.

I'm so freakin' excited about experience

My editorial internship at *Washington Spaces* confirmed my love of writing and the creative process. Although I was researching and writing about luxury homes, which didn't align with my personal interests, it was still a positive learning experience.

My favorite part was sitting in on editorial meetings and popping over to the design team to see the page layout options and cover art pinned to the wall. But my crowning moment during the internship was researching and writing a three-page feature story about high-end doorknobs called "Haute Hardware." I realize that it may not sound like the most riveting journalism, but I took that as a challenge and turned what could be a puff piece into an entertaining article by interviewing artists and architects who specialized in doorknobs. I even went as far as speaking with Hugh Newell Jacobsen, the architect who designed the University of Maryland's Alumni Association building.

It's no surprise at all that I felt inspired to start my own magazine from this singular experience.

When I speak to college students about their fears surrounding the career journey, a big concern they have is the challenge of securing an internship that will help them achieve their passion career. Mia Pearlman, a journalism major at Temple University, shares this sentiment. Not only is she terrified she won't find an internship that will give her the experience she needs, but she also fears "not being able to keep a job" after the fact.

With that in mind, let's walk through how you can secure an internship in a field you're passionate about.

Internships serve as the testing ground for the real world. By dipping your toes in, you gain career experience and discover it's really not so different—and it's pretty freaking fun! But, if it's not, just move on to the next one. There's no point in wasting your time doing something you don't enjoy, especially if it's just an internship. Lesson learned—it's not for you!

> **Pro Tip:**
>
> If you do decide to quit an internship, treat it like a regular job and give two weeks' notice. Quitting respectfully with sincere consideration for the organization is a great skill to practice, and not to mention leaving a positive last impression can result in a helpful future reference, too.

At *College Magazine*, the editor position is a for-credit internship where students lead a team of writers to help shape the direction of *College Magazine's* articles. These students have witnessed their skills transfer directly into their careers. In fact, we invite our graduates back to editorial meetings to share exactly how they apply the skills they learned at *College Magazine* to their current careers.

That's what an internship should do for you—develop skills you can actually use in your life. And if it's not living up to that, ask for more responsibility or take initiative and pitch your own project. We've had students do exactly that at *College Magazine*—see a problem and suggest a solution but also offer to tackle that problem head-on.

Allyson Johnson is the perfect example of a student who hustled for internships with an intentional mindset. Her internship between her junior and senior year ultimately transitioned into her first job that she loved.

While still in school, Allyson knew she was passionate about writing. As early as her freshman year, she reached out to the internship coordinator of the journalism department at her university to learn about local opportunities.

With the coordinator's help, Allyson snagged an internship with Virginia's local *On Tap* magazine. Her role never strayed into the complex—she mainly updated events calendars and wrote small pieces like an article on environmental taxi cabs—but the experience allowed her to get an early foot in the door in a hard-to-crack industry.

Meanwhile, Allyson was still taking advantage of on-campus opportunities like working as an editor, and later editor-in-chief, of the on-campus magazine *Unwind*, and applying for other internships in magazines and newspapers along the way. "You never know what you're going to like and what you're going to be good at," said Allyson.

This mindset landed her internships for both *USA Weekend* magazine and *College Magazine*, where she wrote her first celebrity interview and gained experience editing. Allyson also worked for the university-run newswire, covering education and politics around the D.C. area. She was then accepted to the summer internship program run by the American Society of Magazine Editors. This highly competitive program accepts a mere 40 students from applicants all across the country, sending them to New York to work magazine internships.

Through the American Society of Magazine Editors, Allyson interned at *Rachael Ray Every Day* magazine. Allyson demonstrated her signature extra drive in any challenge she came across and was offered a position at the magazine right after graduating college.

Right off the bat, post-grad, she was working at a lifestyle magazine that she loved. She stayed with the magazine for the next five years. Allyson never had a dull moment at *Rachael Ray*, including writing and editing articles such as discovering bubble gum combinations that taste like cocktails to in-depth travel pieces.

As time went on, Allyson was looking to go back to D.C. and craving a break from the seasonal structure of topics she would cover each year. "I was running out of ways to carve pumpkins...and I was thinking, *What's my next move?*" she said.

She had always wanted a chance to work for National Geographic, and remembered the iconic yellow-bordered magazines stacked in a basket in her family home; she decided to pursue her next career opportunity there. She applied for a position as an editor with *National Geographic's* travel magazine and waited anxiously for a response. Unfortunately, it wasn't what she was hoping for; she wasn't offered the job due to staff changes at the magazine.

"There are rejections along the way," Allyson said. "I've been rejected plenty of times. It's part of life. It only helps you figure out where it is you want to be and what work you have to do to get there."

Even with this setback, Allyson wasn't deterred. She applied to another position at *National Geographic* as an editor in their book department and landed the gig.

All of these circumstances led Allyson to an unexpected position at her dream organization. "I feel like I get to take what I love doing and marry that with this thing that gives back to the world... and that's really what I'm passionate about," she said.

Take a chapter from Allyson's book: By keeping an open mind to a different role, you can get your foot in the door at an organization you love, like *National Geographic*. An added bonus: Once you're at your dream company, it's often easier to move jobs laterally from within than if you are applying from the outside. If you're not seeing an opening that fits at a company you're interested in, start by asking if they can create an internship position for you.

Once you're in the internship, make sure you maximize the experience. You're here to learn, after all. "Just start out being curious about everything. Ask questions," said Claire Kreger-Boaz, senior project manager for NAMM Public Affairs and Government Relations and The NAMM Foundation. The experience Claire creates for college music students and faculty at The NAMM Show, an annual music industry event, is designed to do exactly that—ignite curiosity.

Take it from another expert, Christopher Lochhead, former Silicon Valley chief marketing officer for three major companies. "Train yourself to be a legendary result producer," Christopher said. "Train yourself to be the person that other people want to have on their team because you produce results, and you do it in a powerful way, and you're a great person to partner with, and collaborate with, and get stuff done with."

Christopher Lochhead is a #1 bestselling Amazon author and a #1 Apple business podcaster who now hosts the podcast *Follow Your Different*. In addition to co-authoring two bestselling books, he's been an advisor to over 50 venture-backed startups alongside his CMO experiences.

During your internship, keep your eyes peeled for future opportunities. "Be open to those moments where life taps you on the shoulder and says, *Hey! Over there!* I didn't know that I was going to become a CMO. I was just drawn to marketing and somebody else saw the potential in me. I didn't know that was going to happen; I was on a different path at that point, and that opportunity presented itself," said Christopher.

"The likelihood that whatever is in your mind about your future career, the likelihood that it doesn't turn out that way is very, very high, and that's okay," he said. "In a lot of ways, success is about failing in the right direction."

Grad school or nah?

Does your career vision involve graduate school? These are two main things to consider when deciding whether to continue your education.

Many students about to graduate from undergraduate studies, as well as young professionals in their first job, have asked for my take on graduate school. So here you go, these are my thoughts: There is no one-size-fits-all answer. I do believe there are immense benefits to continued learning no matter what your path, and graduate school may be the answer for you, but that isn't the case for everyone.

Of course, numerous career journeys require a graduate degree. Sometimes the best choice is to attend right after college graduation, especially if the field requires it. For example, higher education positions like university academic advisors or professors, or many research, medical, or technical positions require graduate school.

With that being said, in the case of a Master of Business Administration (MBA), experts often recommend that college grads work an entry-level job in their desired fields before applying so that they can bring that real-world business or engineering knowledge to their MBA cohort environment.

Graduate school is a massive financial and time investment, so do your research before making your decision. Never choose graduate school for the purpose of delaying the career journey or with the sole intention of making more money once you get your degree—remember, money motivation will only get you so far, and a higher degree doesn't always equal a larger salary; in fact, I've heard from several friends who went to law school that while their post-graduate school job did offer a higher pay, they're now stuck with a long burden of paying off debt.

The best way to find out if pursuing a higher degree is the right choice for you is to link up with other people in your desired field and find out if they've taken and recommend that path. Learn from employers you hope to work for if graduate school is key for your career. From there, determine for yourself if it fits with your passion.

Everyday I'm hustlin'

For quite some time, *College Magazine* was my side hustle. It didn't emerge as a fully-fledged business. It was my passion and a hobby business.

A side hustle can be any project that earns you money. But for those that use that time and energy to execute a passion project, it becomes more than just about the money—it becomes an experience that demonstrates and grows your dedication to your passion.

"One key thing that I look for is initiative and hustle," said Rajni Roshan, senior technical program manager at Amazon. "It speaks volumes of your work ethic, even if you don't have a long list of work experiences on your resume."

Rajni has over a decade of experience in the tech industry under her belt and is passionate about technology solutions that have a social impact. As the program director of Girls in Tech San Diego, a nonprofit focused on supporting women in tech, Rajni's a strong advocate for young girls and women in STEM. She also regularly takes time out of her schedule to mentor other women in the industry.

Previously Rajni was managing a technical Program called STIP (Smart Transportation Innovation Program) at the University of California, San Diego, collaborating with city officials, larger companies as well as startups, and the University to drive smart, safe and sustainable transportation innovation in southern California. Prior to that, at IBM in the UK, Rajni worked with her team to help clients like the Wimbledon tennis tournament solve their challenges with design-thinking strategies (the process by which design concepts are created). Leveraging her degree in computer engineering and her years of experience at IBM leading a team, she designed unique tech solutions and created test pilot versions for her clients combining existing and new technology.

She went from software developer to working on business and customer focused roles at IBM in mergers and acquisitions and client solution design. "I've always followed what I've been most interested in," said Rajni. "I knew that I didn't want to stay a developer all my life and I tried to find ways to get closer to my (next) goal."

These new career opportunities within IBM, and since, didn't just fall into Rajni's lap. "I looked out, I reached out, I found out about what else was going on, and I started chasing down those opportunities," she said.

And when it comes to new hires, she's looking for candidates that can make an impression with stories that demonstrate their work ethic—projects they've worked on outside of the classroom (a.k.a. side hustles).

Carey Smolensky started his side hustle as a DJ in high school by working private events such as Bar Mitzvahs. Later he attended Loyola University in Chicago on the path toward dental school.

He aced his DATs (dental aptitude tests) and was accepted to dental school after three years of undergrad. But by that point Carey had fallen in love with his on-campus radio experience and was continuing to build his DJ business. He realized that he felt more passionately about his side hustle than his studies and that his entertainment company had a lot of growth potential.

Carey said he had a realization: "I'm going into debt because I'm pursuing [dentistry] and I have a business that wants to grow—which is my passion—and it can't because I'm going into debt, all the while thinking I'm doing something I don't want to do." He officially decided to pursue his growing business over dentistry. This wasn't an easy decision, but he made the leap and never looked back.

"My parents weren't big fans when I told them I was going to change the Dr. into a DJ…"

As Carey had envisioned, his production company, Carey Smolensky Productions, evolved into a business providing sound, video, lighting, set design, keynote speakers, and talent for global conferences. Life as a CEO of a fast-moving business is a hustle. Carey says an average day in his job is "similar to a boxing ring."

"It's constant—it's not just nine to five. It's a mindset, and you're always fighting to stay alive."

On any given day, you can find Carey contracting and communicating with strategic partners, planning events, overseeing logistics, or working on his grassroots initiative, A Warmer Winter, or other charities he is involved with such as Front Row Foundation and Angel Wings International. In other words, Carey has quite a few passions, which has sparked side hustles, including volunteering to help others in need.

Need more side hustle inspiration than that?

While still in school, Marty Ringlein side hustled by creating the digital Greek Yearbook on his campus. This experience was a taste of what his future career could look like in the creative web development and design industry, launching his own agency.

Melissa Eisler began her career journey as a writer and an editor for an online publisher that focused on health and wellness. While there, as a side hustle, she started leading workshops around mindfulness for leaders and stress management in the corporate setting. She also decided to return to school and get a master's degree in leadership, and now has a private leadership and executive coaching practice.

Will Hansen took on his first website project for a tequila importing company as a side hustle while in school at the Art Institute. This helped him build his portfolio and led to his first paid internship.

Side hustles don't have to just be for fun or extra cash flow; they can help you gain hands-on experience, make connections, and get a stronger foothold in your desired career. Most importantly, they demonstrate your passion in a tangible way.

Volunteering: the G.O.A.T

Clubs and organizations spark new experiences and skill sets and help you grow in your passion while expanding your social circle. Another way to do this is by volunteering your time. And the best part of volunteering? You get to make a difference in the world.

There are many different forms of volunteering other than spending time at a soup kitchen. You can volunteer by fundraising, such as running a marathon for your favorite cause, or by donating your time, like meeting one-on-one with a student after school to offer free SAT tutoring. Find something you support, volunteer your time there, and stick with it.

Having consistency in what you volunteer for is important. It shows you're interested in making a long-term impact in a specific area and aren't just volunteering for every disconnected cause that comes your way.

I've always enjoyed giving my time to young people in education. That's why I volunteer as a tutor and mentor, especially for students in low-income communities whose parents can't afford to pay a tutor when their kid may be falling behind in their academics.

While working my first job out of college, I volunteered at a local middle school through a tutoring program in Arlington, Virginia. Then, while running *College Magazine* full-time, I volunteered at a nearby elementary school in Rockville, Maryland. Later, when I moved to Washington, D.C., I joined the Network for Teaching Entrepreneurship and helped a high school student develop her business idea and pitch for a student business competition. Even when I was volunteering for just one hour a week, I found that the impact on these young students—and within myself—was exponential.

Today, even while I run CollegeMagazine.com and write this book, I dedicate two hours of my week to students at Reality Changers and have been an actively involved volunteer over the last three years. Committing at that level allows you to make an impact that you can *feel*. For me, I get so much joy out of the experience of watching my students achieve higher GPAs or submit their college applications with confidence.

Volunteering feeds your hangry soul in many ways. You learn that you have a lot to offer when you give your time to someone who needs your help. You also gain communication skills and innumerable transferable career skills depending on the nature of the organization.

Especially if you are interested in making a career change from the corporate world to the nonprofit world, having volunteer experience is critical to setting yourself apart when applying to a job in a field in which you might have zero formal experience.

Lisa Rosenfelt's passion career was inspired by her volunteer efforts. Today she is the co-owner of Ivy Street, a co-working space. In her free time, she volunteers as the managing director of Girls in Tech San Diego and is motivated by her passion for helping women thrive in the local tech industry.

"One of the biggest passions I have is to create opportunities for women and underrepresented groups to join these industries, tech and entrepreneurship, and get the support and leg up they need to be successful," said Lisa.

Lisa began her career journey studying neuroscience at the University of California San Diego and went on to get a Ph.D. in neurolinguistics. During her doctoral program, she realized her true passion didn't exactly align with a career in research. Instead, she was happiest when she was orchestrating community events for her peers.

"If I was being honest, probably the biggest value I brought to my doctoral program was in planning the open house weekends and the community involvement pieces and the parts where all the grad students gathered for brunch and studied together so that we didn't feel so lost and alone," Lisa said.

However, after graduation, Lisa chose to follow a linear path, taking on a postdoctoral position in research. But after just two years, her passion pulled her back to the idea of community.

"It really started with…going to different organizations and meetups and meeting people and volunteering my time and seeing what was available in the community," she said. This passion for community and volunteering led her to opportunities such as Girls in Tech where, after starting as a volunteer, she has now taken on a leadership role.

"Showing up and doing the things you say you are going to do, making the commitment, and following through is one of the most significant things you can do to show not just your passion but your ability to be trusted and moved up the ladder into leadership," Lisa said.

So how can you get more involved in your community? Learn from Lisa and seek opportunities where your strengths can shine.

When you begin or change your career, you want to show where your values lie and communicate what causes you're passionate about. Look back at the causes you listed way back in Chapter 3 and start thinking about how you can get involved. We all have the ability to make a difference in the world—what better way to show this than by volunteering?

Now, how much time should you spend volunteering? There's no right or wrong answer. Giving back to your community in any shape or form is important, even if that means one trip a year to the Salvation Army to help organize gifts for the holidays or volunteering at your local senior center over Thanksgiving. However, dedicating an ongoing amount of time to a cause speaks volumes. It shows your commitment. And you get to watch the difference you make in the world unfold. Now, *that's* an impactful story to tell.

In addition to local organizations in your community, here are 10 organizations that have local chapters or nationwide volunteering opportunities to help you gain experience, give back, support an important cause, and make an impact:

- Charity: Water
- Camfed
- She Should Run
- The National Immigration Law Center
- The Trevor Project
- Sierra club
- Propublica
- Black Lives Matter
- Center for Community Change
- Coalition to Stop Gun Violence

ACTION:

Which volunteer opportunities align with your passion? What steps can you take next to join or get involved? Write it down!

7

MAKE THE FIRST MOVE

Have you ever done something that scares you, like passing that note to the kid in your fifth grade class to see if they want to go out with you? *Circle YES or NO.*

How about asking your co-worker how to fax something, or giving a big class presentation? Does the thought of any of these scenarios make you break out into a cold sweat? Connecting with people can be nerve-wracking. It requires *a lot* of courage.

And I'm not going to lie and promise you it gets better with time because sometimes it doesn't. I've been facing these fears for years—and I consider myself an extrovert. To this day I still get nervous sending a LinkedIn message or email to someone I admire. Hitting that "Send" button makes me panic. But it has to get done—whether it's sending an email to a big brand for a partnership opportunity, reaching out to a former classmate to network, or yes, sending that cutie a DM. Sure, it's scary, but the end result is either something positive or radio silence; either way, there's nothing to lose.

Pro Tip:

Go into your Gmail settings and enable "undo send," a tool that allows you a 5-30 second opportunity to retract your emails after hitting send. This comes in handy for those times when you forget to add an important detail or you spell a name wrong. This button has saved me so many times. Plus, it helps take the edge off the fear of hitting send.

I tell you this not to scare you but to let you know that it's totally normal if you get this feeling, too. It's also good to know that when you connect intentionally and hit the "send" button, you have just separated yourself from everyone else who was too afraid to reach out. And that's no small feat.

You've done the hard work of unlocking within yourself and seeking out opportunities; now it's time to achieve your passion career by connecting courageously. It's time to set yourself apart.

I'm not going to promise you that you'll hear back from everyone you reach out to. Quite frankly, you'll probably get a lot of crickets. But don't let the silence deter you.

I'll never forget how my parents encouraged me to send a copy of *College Magazine* along with a personal letter to Cathy Black, head of Hearst Magazines and creator of *The Oprah Magazine*. I had just read her book *Basic Black* and, since I ran a startup magazine, she was someone I admired. Talk about reaching out to someone in the limelight—she was well into her career, totally crushing it, and totally out of my league.

I wrote the letter, agonizingly edited it, and sent it off. Did I hear back? Unfortunately, no.

But am I glad I did it? Most definitely.

The simple act of writing a letter and boldly reaching out made all the difference. I didn't know it at the time, but I was practicing for all the other people I would eventually try to contact. It made me incredibly nervous to take that first step with Cathy, but I proved to myself that I could do it.

And to this day, all my most fantastic achievements stem from the moments when I felt nervous but I mustered up the courage to move forward anyway.

Like my Cathy Black face-plant moment, I'll never forget the time I met Chelsea Handler and asked for an interview. She was in Washington, D.C. for a signing of her new book, *Chelsea Chelsea Bang Bang*. My best friend Kari and I arrived early to get a good spot...but we certainly underestimated the rest of her fans. By the time we got there, an hour before the signing, the line was already out the door and around the block. We were stuck behind hundreds of fans waiting for our turn to meet Chelsea.

At this point I had been running *College Magazine* for two years and we were getting celebrity interviews left and right, with actors from shows like *Glee*, *Gossip Girl*, and *Modern Family*. (Keep in mind this was 2010. When it came to attracting college students to a print magazine, celebrities were absolutely necessary.)

As a personal Chelsea fan, I had tried over and over to get in touch—but to no avail. She was kind of a big deal and extremely hard to reach...that was until I read online about her local book signing. I saw this as my one shot. Prepared with a couple magazines and a hand-written note, I stood in line and waited.

I felt nervous. Obviously, I was about to meet *the* Chelsea Handler and ask her for an exclusive interview in *College Magazine*. After an agonizing wait, Kari and I advanced far enough in line to the point where I could see Chelsea sitting at her signing table with her team shuffling along her hordes of fans. As I inched closer to the moment of truth, I noticed that Chelsea barely had any time to even look up at the person in front of her as she was signing. She was just scribbling her name as quickly as she could and moving on to the next. This made sense, seeing as there were over 400 people there, but my heart sank, nonetheless.

Still, I knew I *had* to say something. I needed to make an impression.

Channeling my inner Chelsea (having read her first two books and seen every episode her show, I had a sense of her mindset), I thought about what would catch her attention. And suddenly it hit me—I knew exactly what to say. The thought of it alone made me so anxious that I began to break into a visible sweat. I knew it was a crazy idea, but it was the only thing I could think of to catch Chelsea's attention.

When my turn finally came to stumble up to the table, I mustered up all my confidence. I took a deep breath. And finally, with nothing to lose, I blurted out: "Chelsea, you look f*cking hot."

Chelsea paused with her pen hovering in midair over an open book. After a beat, she looked up at me, smiled the biggest smile, and said, "Thank you!"

And, of course, it was true; she looked killer. It was no lie. But the signing line was moving so quickly that I knew your average compliment would go unnoticed. My bold statement, coupled with that touch of vulgarity that Chelsea appreciates, *definitely* caught her attention.

I couldn't believe it. I was having a conversation with Chelsea Handler. But I didn't have time to bask in it—with adrenaline rushing through my veins and without a second to waste, I quickly handed her the stack of magazines I'd brought and replied, "I'm Amanda Nachman, I run College Magazine, and I would love to interview you for our next issue."

Imagine how shocked I was when she said yes.

We were ushered away from the line, and Chelsea's assistant Eva gave me her business card to schedule the interview. I took her card and left the bookstore in a daze. I had made a courageous connection, with *Chelsea Handler* of all people, and it had actually worked.

It wasn't so easy afterwards. There were countless email threads and missed calls as I chased down an interview appointment. This was Chelsea Handler, after all; she was a busy and successful woman, and I represented a regional print magazine with only 120,000 readers at the time.

But after following up for weeks, we heard back from Eva with a date and time and finally confirmed our interview with Chelsea. It was well worth the struggle. The interview ended up being hilarious and very Chelsea, and was, of course, our cover story. One of my favorite moments from the interview still makes me laugh to this day:

College Magazine: Any advice for college girls aspiring to lead your renaissance-like life?

Chelsea Handler: Know when to leave a party before you embarrass yourself.

Chelsea is one of my most courageous connections, and even now I'm still reaching out to people who make me nervous. It doesn't get less scary with experience. But you will get better at it—and remember that connecting is necessary to achieving your passion career.

Let your passion fuel you to step outside of your comfort zone and connect. Remember, what *is* the worst that could happen?

Get their attention

So, you've identified what you want. Now it's time to identify who's already got it. When you meet someone that's doing what you desire to do, you can learn from and get inspired by them.

You spend the majority of your time in your comfort zone: going to restaurants you have already eaten at, talking to people you already know, doing the work you're familiar with. Now is the time to get *un*comfortable. Doing what you know will only deliver the same results. If you want something new, you have to do something new.

I'm not saying cold call a celebrity right this second. Start small with someone one step ahead of you in their career path, or someone at your level and experience but who might be working for a company you admire. By making these small connections, you're practicing and preparing for future larger connections.

"It's the tiny steps that get you there," said Gail Kraft, founder of The Empowering Process. "When you take tiny steps, while still looking far ahead, you don't realize how far you come."

And you're reading this book because you want exceptional results—passion career results. Results like that aren't going to happen on their own.

Start making courageous connections by making a list. As you can tell at this point, I'm a big fan of lists, because when you see something written down on paper (like the name of your dream career connection) you are one step closer to actually bringing that list to life. If you just keep these lists in your head, they live in the intangible.

Once your list of dream connections is written in ink, contemplate how you'll approach them; you don't need something as concrete as a magazine interview as a reason to reach out. Simply asking to meet with someone for the sake of learning about their life and career trajectory is enough. Take it from Rajni Roshen of Amazon and Girls in Tech San Diego.

"You don't have to be able to give someone your skills, or your time or your advice in order to receive that back. It can happen the other way. Just ask. What's the worst that can happen? Ask for time to ask a few questions," said Rajni.

Let's say you're passionate about videos games and you've embraced your inner nerd. You've unlocked your passion and set a career vision to write video game storylines featuring characters who want to solve the world's greatest environmental challenges, all with an end goal to inspire young people. Meanwhile you've started getting intentional with your experiences by joining your on-campus eSports club and writing for their website. You've even started doing your research and found that Blizzard Entertainment, the creator of your favorite video game of all time, is based in Southern California near your college—so you've applied to their student internship! With all of that under your belt, you're prepared to connect courageously.

YOUR PROFILE

INTERESTS
World of Warcraft, StarCraft, and EverQuest video games

STRENGTHS
Writing, creativity

VALUES
Authenticity, fairness, environmental issues

VISION
To write video game storylines featuring characters who want to solve the world's greatest environmental challenges to inspire young people

INTENTIONAL EXPERIENCES
San Diego State University's eSports club blog manager

IN PROGRESS
Applying to Blizzard Entertainment's student summer internship program

The first step to connecting courageously is actually going to find those connections. I took an hour and looked up video game companies in San Diego and found Daybreak Game Company, Juggernaut Games, and Psyonix. From there I went to LinkedIn and looked at the employees in roles that involved creative writing.

Pro Tip:

If you don't have a LinkedIn account yet, it's about time to create one. It's totally fine if your profile is just a photo of you and your university for now. As we move into the next chapter, you'll be creating your personal brand and building upon this page—but for the purpose of connecting with potential mentors, you simply need an initial account.

For example, I found Rob Chestney, the lead narrative designer and writer at Daybreak Game Company. *Wow*, he's living your dream career. According to Rob's LinkedIn profile, he could be a potential mentor for you. He graduated from Berkeley in film and communications and has 20 years of storytelling and writing experience. Just imagine speaking with Rob and learning about his career journey. How incredible would it be to have him in your corner, rooting for your success in achieving your passion career?

Don't let those 20 years of experience in the field shake you; Rob might be thrilled to hear from a young professional like you. But at the same time, don't put all your eggs in Rob's basket—he's a busy dude. Before you write to one potential mentor, identify at least five other people in your passion career industry. It's always good to have options. You could also consider reaching out to someone in an assistant or mid-level position. Someone earlier in their career may be able to give you more time than someone with senior responsibilities.

ACTION:

Jot down five inspirational people in your passion career.

Once you have your list of five, it's time to make moves and reach out. Here's an example letter you can write Rob. On LinkedIn, you have to get concise because of the 300-word limit (to send a message to someone on LinkedIn, click "Connect" on their profile and then opt-in to include a personal message). But if you can find a connection's email address from their company website or their personal website, you can write a letter like this:

Dear Rob,

How are you? I write for my campus' eSports club's website and I'm a major EverQuest fan. I saw that you're the Lead Narrative Designer & Writer at Daybreak and I am so impressed with your career.

I would be honored to learn more about your career journey. Are you available for a 15-minute call on Thursday at 2:00 p.m. or Friday between 12:00 - 5:00 p.m. this week?

I look forward to hearing from you!

Sincerely,
Amanda

In the message, it's important to include the following:

1. A friendly approach, like "How are you?"
2. Some basic information about you and your passion.
3. A sincere compliment. This shows you've done your research and that you are inspired by their work.
4. The concrete ask: 15 minutes of their time.
5. Specificity or a deadline to your ask. If you reach out without mentioning a specific time, there's no urgency for someone to get back to you.

Pro Tip:

How many emails have you started with "My name is...."? And don't lie. I see college students start their emails with this all the time! We've all done it—but this is a rookie mistake. Professionals never begin with their name because it's in their signature, so you end up looking like you've never sent an email before in your life. Don't be that guy. You want to be concise and get right to the point. So, skip the "My name is" nonsense, and never bring it back.

Let's say sending a note like this terrifies you. That's okay! You're not alone. Reaching out cold to someone new is nerve-wracking. But truly, what's the worst that can happen? You can either get a yes, a no, a maybe, or you might not ever hear back at all. No harm done. The upside of the yes is worth it.

Macey Spensley, the editor in chief at my new website College-Vested (remember how I told you I was multi-passionate?), which helps students tackle big financial decisions about credit cards, student loans, and auto insurance, had to overcome her shyness when it came to contacting financial experts for her articles. She quickly learned that, like most things in life, practice makes you better.

"You eventually stop worrying about what the other person may think of you," said Macey.

If you don't hear back in two to three days, send a follow-up email. Here's an example of how that email can look:

```
Dear Rob,

How are you? I wanted to circle back on my
last email.

I would love to learn about your career
journey. Are you available for a 15-minute
call next week?

I look forward to hearing from you!

Sincerely,
Amanda
```

Sometimes it takes two or even three emails to show that you are committed to connecting.

If you would feel more comfortable having an excuse to reach out, then create one. I have a podcast, which gives me a perfect excuse to contact people in their passion careers—especially people I admire. Then I get to interview them.

The best part about interviewing people for my podcast is that I get to discover more about the person and make a connection in the process. When you ask someone questions about their experiences and are genuinely curious—and, more importantly, demonstrate that curiosity—you learn much more about them. A deeper connection grows from this experience. This is how we build trust.

Think about the countless hours you've spent hanging out with your squad—the trips to the mall, the nights spent playing video games at each other's houses, the afternoon hikes, and millions of Snapchats. It takes hours, days, and years to develop the kind of trust you've created with your BFF. Networking and building meaningful relationships with mentors require that same foundation of trust. Be patient when making new connections. You don't have to text them all the details about your awkward date last night like you might text your BFF, but understand that all relationships, even mentorships, take time.

After each podcast recording, I take a moment to thank my interviewee and we reflect on the podcast session. It's in these last few trust-filled moments that I have some of the most profound conversations with the people I interview. It's because we've spent an hour learning from one another and sharing experiences. This connects us in a way that isn't always as achievable in everyday interactions like grabbing a meal or coffee.

When you set aside time to interview someone or simply give someone your full attention, you really get to know them. And vice versa. It's a fantastic feeling to connect intentionally.

I honestly believe that attention—*full* attention—is the currency of our time. It's the most valuable thing you can give or receive.

Did you know that there is scientific evidence that proves even just the presence of your cell phone during a physical conversation affects the conversation itself? According to MIT professor Sherry Turkle, we're more likely to hold surface level conversations if a cell phone is on the table.[18] Why is this? Subconsciously we're preparing for the moment that phone rings, so we keep things light where the conversation can easily be paused for a potential call.

I know, mortifying. What a shame to think about how many times we have our cell phones present when we're talking to someone else. Think about all the missed deep connections.

This is why I believe that full attention, without distractions, is one of the most precious gifts today.

Anyone—yes, even you—can create a podcast a blog or any kind of reason to interview someone, just like I do. I would encourage you to start your podcast, blog, Tumblr, or YouTube channel today. We all have access to these platforms, so why not use it to your advantage to build your personal brand?

Struggling to think of a topic for your new blog? How about "Everything You Ever Wanted to Know About _____." Fill in the blank with your passion or career industry.

Remember though, you don't need a podcast or an excuse to interview someone you admire. An 18-year-old high school student I worked with at Reality Changers, Bonnie Nguyen, made a courageous connection that completely blew me away

At the time, though, she didn't even realize she'd done anything out of the ordinary. I was helping her on one of the sections of her college application in which she was writing out her internship and involvement experiences. One of the experiences listed was the following: "Research Assistant: Worked in the lab using the Mind Ware Technology. Collected and analyzed data. Worked for the summer with professor and graduate students."

This piqued my interest and left me with a ton of questions. *What was this lab? What kind of research? How did you get involved?*

When I talked to Bonnie about her research assistant position, as it turned out there was much more to the story. One day after school she was reading an article in *The New York Times* about a study on honesty. She's passionate about positive psychology, helping people create better habits and flourish, which was why she found herself reading the article in the first place.

But what Bonnie did next surprised me most. She took action. She searched online for contact information for Professor Oveis, who was featured in the article for his research on emotions at University of California San Diego. And then she emailed him.

"Wait a minute, you just went for it? You emailed him?" I asked her. I was stunned that she made such a bold move. Bonnie didn't even bat an eye. She matter-of-factly told me that she was so interested in what Professor Oveis was doing that she couldn't help but reach out.

In the email she asked to meet with him and discuss his research and the opportunities in his lab. Professor Oveis agreed, and after their conversation he created a lab position just for her.

Now *that's* impressive—talk about a courageous connection! Most students wouldn't have even considered writing an email or—*gasp*—clicking send.

But more importantly, she was following a passion. Bonnie's passion aligned with the professor's research and that was what ultimately compelled her to take that next step.

With this incredible background story in mind, we transformed her college application description. Even within the bounds of the word-count limit, we ended up with something pretty striking:

"After reading Professor Oveis' *New York Time's* article, I contacted and interviewed to create a research position in his empathy study. I cleaned up and analyzed heart rate variability data, learned how to use Mind Ware Technologies Ltd.'s HRV Analysis Software, and worked closely with professor and graduate student team."

And right now, Bonnie's college acceptance letters are rolling in.

A DM every day

Whether Bonnie realized it then or not, when she met with Professor Oveis, she was conducting an informational interview. It was as simple as that; she set up a meeting with no strings attached. Her intention was genuine. She wanted to learn, gather information, share her passion, and create a connection with a person whose work she admired.

If Bonnie can do it, so can you! Then, if all works out like it did for her, you not only learn about something you're interested in, but you can also gain a new cheerleader in your corner. *Ready? Okay!* This person is rooting for you. They are impressed with your passion, invested in your success, and most likely interested in helping you succeed. Just like Professor Oveis felt inspired to create a position in his lab for Bonnie, you too could have new opportunities open up through your courageous connections.

When you have an informational interview and create a positive relationship with someone, that person may start connecting you to job openings or other professionals in your industry who can help you on your career journey. And they're very likely open to giving you feedback along the way. There are no guarantees here, of course, but your connection may be open to helping you beyond just talking about their experience.

If this sounds like a mentorship to you, then *ding ding ding* you are spot on. I've been asked many times before, "how do I find a mentor?" An informational interview can be a great gateway to a promising mentorship.

Why did Professor Oveis want to work with Bonnie? Because when he met her, she spoke her passion and it connected directly with his own. Imagine meeting a younger version of yourself. Let's say you love to skateboard, and your 10-year-old neighbor has always wanted to learn. Wouldn't you be more likely to help her because you share the same passion?

With a mentorship in mind, make sure you're making the most of the informational interview experience. But after you've landed the interview—which means you've followed the steps above and have a general sense of your potential mentor—what's the next step?

First, go back and review everything you learned about this person when you were reaching out. Then, dig even deeper. You want to show that you took the time to learn about them and that you're taking their time seriously. Because this is someone you admire, they've probably been in their career for a decent amount of time and have an online footprint that allows you to research them. At the very least they have a LinkedIn profile where you can do some good old-fashioned internet stalking. For example, you can study a bit more about their alma mater, the companies they've worked for, and any organizations with which they're affiliated.

Write this information down. This could be as simple as three to five bullet points on this person's education and employment history. Then brainstorm questions you want to ask about this person's specific career journey. Here are 10 questions to get you started:

1. What did you imagine your career path being during college at _____ and after?

2. How did you first get your foot in the door at _____?

3. Describe a day in your life in your career today as a _____.

4. What are some of your favorite parts of what you get to do as a _____?

5. How did you discover your passion for _____?

6. How has following your passion for _____ impacted your life?

7. What career advice can you share for someone like me, also passionate about _____?

8. How do you feel you've set yourself apart from other applicants along your career journey?

9. Are there any organizations you are part of that have been helpful in achieving your career goals?

10. What do you and your company look for when it comes to hiring someone at _____ ?

You may not cover all your questions in 15 minutes and that's okay! I highly recommend ranking these questions in order of what you're most interested in learning, just in case you aren't able to get to them all. And, of course, if the conversation takes off naturally, feel free to step away from the Q&A format. In actuality, that off-the-cuff conversation may be more valuable than any question you could ask. Go with the flow—you'll likely end up building that meaningful and authentic relationship you're looking for.

But whether you stick to your script or not, pay close attention that you're really demonstrating that you've done your homework. Imagine you have spent 20 years in your dream career, have won awards, and have even been featured in magazines—and then along comes a 20-something who didn't even spend more than 10 minutes reading about you. They ask questions like, "How did you get started in your job?" versus, "When I saw your first prototype and realized how much your style has evolved over the last 20 years, I was so impressed! How did you first know you wanted to pursue fashion design?"

The former says "slacker," and the latter says "passionate." Asking unique, specific questions shows that you are genuinely curious; you took the time to research them and come up with something thoughtful to ask.

When I'm meeting someone and I want to fully understand what they do, I remain curious and ask questions even after learning their job title and elevator pitch description. When people ask me, "What do you do?" and they hear that I'm the publisher at *College Magazine*, rarely do they follow up with more questions. They assume they know what this means. But more often than not, you have no idea what another person's career looks like from the outside. You're blind to what they do on a day-to-day basis. You have no idea if they're sitting at a desk, in meetings, traveling to client sites, or hosting events. The only way to really learn is to ask them to break it down. Get them to paint you a picture. *What did yesterday look like for you? What's your morning routine? Do you work with a team or on more solo projects? Is your job stressful or more relaxed?*

I cannot tell you how many people I meet who assume that, as the publisher of *College Magazine*, I write articles every day. Most people don't fully understand the ins and outs of the publishing business and so they gravitate to the one thing they do know: the final visible product, which is the articles. But that's like assuming every employee who works for Microsoft builds computers.

When someone asks me follow up questions like those above, they learn so much more about what it takes to run *College Magazine*. They'll discover that I am in charge of the business, marketing, and operations side of the magazine.

On a more holistic level, they'll understand my mindset as a leader and learn how I achieve success—like how I believe in the power of a morning routine, sparked by reading Hal Elrod's book, *The Miracle Morning*. Ever since I reluctantly began following Hal's advice to remove the snooze option from my routine, I've felt more energized and productive throughout my day.

My day starts like this—I roll out of bed and I read. I start off every day reading (mostly nonfiction) because it's something I love doing and I look forward to learning something new first thing in the morning. Right now, I'm reading *White Hot Truth* by Danielle LaPorte. I'm also reading *Launch* by Jeff Walker, and I'm learning new methods to launch this very book in the most strategic way possible to elevate readership and drive exposure.

Once I've read, I'll write in my journal to get my new ideas down on paper. If I've given myself enough time, (which isn't likely) I'll strike a few yoga poses and stretch before officially kicking off my workday.

By 9:00 a.m. I'm meeting with Celina, our Editorial Director, to hear about her projects and team communications. She'll share progress on new initiatives, like our series on the top 100 cities for study abroad (articles that dive into the universities you can attend in a specific city abroad and what the experience looks and feels like from students who have been there).

Afterwards, I connect with our advertisers to discuss campaign progress. For instance, our campaign with the company Wolf Scooters has currently reached millions of students through a scooter giveaway and we've featured their brand in popular articles about the most scooter-friendly campuses and best scooter shops across the country.

This is just a glimpse of what a career position breakdown might look like if you take the time to ask specific questions. Don't you feel more informed about what a publisher actually does after hearing this? I'd think so!

Set yourself apart by asking for the breakdown. No matter what you do, ask follow-up questions during an informational interview before you dive into any stories about yourself. It's tempting to turn the tables and humbly brag about our own lives, but challenge yourself to first get curious about the person you're speaking to.

Jon Vroman, motivational speaker, author, and founder of Front Row Foundation, encourages people to always ask three questions that dig deeper. How often, when we're presented with, for example, a travel hiccup story, do we then feel the urge to share our own sagas of lost luggage—when instead we could get a little more curious and dive deeper with follow-up questions? *"Wow, I can't believe that layover. How were your adventures in Thailand? Which beach was your favorite? What surprised you most?"*

Wouldn't *you* love to always be asked three more questions? It feels good to know that the person listening to you is genuinely interested in what you have to say.

Here are some example "dig deeper" questions:

- What does a day in your career look like?
- What do you enjoy most about your current position?
- What have been some of your challenges you've faced?
- What surprised you the most about your experience?
- How have you grown in your role?
- What are some of your goals for your career?

Andrea Stone held an essential informational interview on her path to becoming a school counselor. In a moment of reflection, Andrea recalled how much her high school counselor helped with her college application process and how much she had inspired her. She remembered turning to her counselor any time she received a college rejection letter or felt stressed about her future. With that in mind, Andrea decided to reach out.

Her school counselor was thrilled to hear from Andrea and was eager to meet with her to share what her career was like. That conversation further confirmed for Andrea that she was passionate about helping young people. Andrea then embarked on her intentional career journey by interning at a small summer camp. From there, she applied to three alternative teaching programs for her first job after college. The rest is history.

Imagine how flattered you would feel, like Andrea's former school counselor, if someone cared to hear about your career. That warm feeling is exactly what it feels like to be on the receiving end of an informational interview request email or call. Put yourself in the shoes of the person receiving that request—it's a good feeling, I promise!

Any time you feel nervous about reaching out to someone, remember that your request represents an authentic compliment.

I said it once and I'll say it again: Reach out and speak your passion! You never know what can happen.

I highly recommend arranging informational interviews over Zoom or another video conferencing tool if you can't meet in person. If you don't have a dedicated desk for video interviews, you may consider placing a chair by a window or nicely decorated wall and then placing your laptop on a stack of books in order to create a professional looking background. That way the focus is on you. I can't tell you how many students we've interviewed over Zoom in a darkly lit, messy bedroom.

Ensure that your location will be quiet and if you have roommates, remind them in advance that you'll be in an interview. Dress the part too—business casual at least— so that you're feeling very boss like. Be sure to log into Zoom the day before to test out your background, lighting, and audio, and to ensure that your face is centered on the screen. You can even ask a friend to confirm that your video is on point. These steps create a stellar first impression. Now it's time to light up the screen with your passion, yes you! Show up energized.

"Most things happen because of the network and the relationships that are built," said Kristin, so make sure the relationships you're building are as strong as possible by meeting someone face-to-face, IRL or virtual. Not to mention, it's a lot easier to follow up with someone by email after you've met in person. I have found that both parties are more likely to stay in touch. Once they see that you're a real, flesh-and-blood person, they're more likely to be invested in your success and to take an active role.

In fact, that was very much the case for my relationship with Kristin when we started working together on the 50by2050 Project. I drove up to Los Angeles to attend Ignite's Young Women Run event and this in-person connection made all the difference in us staying in touch and growing our partnership. Then I interviewed her using Zoom video for my podcast.

Since then, Kristin and I have launched incredible giveaways for Ignite's events and we're currently working together on The 50by2050 Project. Who knows how we would have ultimately partnered together if we'd only ever connected over email—but I'm willing to bet we'd be collaborating on a much smaller scale.

Now that you've prepared for the informational interview by doing your research and developing thoughtful questions, don't forget to arrive to the interview as your authentic self. You're probably thinking, *Wait, what? Who else would I arrive as?* But you would be surprised how many of us put on an act, playing out a version of ourselves that we believe the other person wants us to be.

Often, we're just nervous and aiming to please, hoping to say the "right" things. But remember—this is for informational purposes only. This isn't even a job interview.

And even if it were a "real" interview, don't forget that we're all just humans who want to connect with one another. As much as you might be tempted to project the perfect candidate, try to resist that urge.

Christine DiDonato, founder of Career Revolution and Awesome-Boss.com, shares this sentiment. "Companies that are interviewing you have seen it all. What they're really looking for is authenticity," she said. "When I've interviewed people and they come in and they seem relaxed, they smile, and they simply tell me, here's who I am, here's what I do well, here are some things I've struggled with, here's what I want to learn, [that's authenticity]," said Christine. She also shared that getting to know a candidate on an authentic, personal level helps build trust, which can sometimes supersede the resume.

Remember though, the informational interview isn't a guise to get the job; it isn't a clever way to ask someone for their time and then follow up with: "Will you hire me?" The goal of the informational interview is to, you guessed it, gather information. You're building a relationship with someone in a career you admire. Will doors open for you in the future? Perhaps. Could the relationship lead to a job? Fingers crossed. But that should never be your intended goal. Instead, approach an informational interview with the intention to learn and connect.

At the end of the informational interview, you may decide to ask for suggestions on the next steps you could take in your career journey, or even ask for referrals on other people to contact. Or you may simply ask if you can stay in touch, follow up down the line, or send your resume. Your closing should be whatever feels right. If there was a strong connection, it makes sense to ask to stay in touch or to ask for tangible help like feedback on your resume or recommendations for opportunities in the field.

But most importantly, don't forget the golden rule and say "thank you!" Say it in person or at the close of your call, and even follow up with an email as well to thank them for their time.

Who are 10 people you would love to interview to learn more about their careers? Start by thinking about people you already know but haven't connected with intentionally. It never hurts to start with less courageous connections—ones more easily accessible or less intimidating—to give yourself some practice. For example, consider your university network, professors, friends of friends, students who ran clubs on your campus, parent's friends, cousins who have careers you admire, and more.

Then look on your LinkedIn feed to see what people are doing. Notice what sparks your curiosity. Just imagine if you spent 20 minutes per day like this, looking for people in careers you didn't know much about and reaching out.

Andrea Fitzgerald is doing just that.

Each day Andrea reaches out to one woman in a field that leverages creative writing. She initially wanted to understand what options were out there, including the responsibilities and nuances of different roles she didn't know much about. For example, what does an associate producer at a broadcast company actually do? What is the typical day-to-day of someone in media? "But what I really appreciated was the connections I made with these women," Andrea said. "All of them were older, successful, and busy, which I thought would be intimidating or—at the very least—lead to a lot of ghosting and missed connections. Instead, each of them were engaged, kind, and open about deeply personal aspects of their professional and personal lives."

Through her informational interviews, Andrea learned what each woman liked and didn't like about her job, her future plans for her career, financial stressors, interviewing tips, and more. Best of all, she created a career network.

"I felt more inspired and less lonely," she said. "Often, the job search is a solitary process—we don't ask family or friends to look over our cover letters, we don't reach out to professors or bosses to mentor us, we don't leverage any sort of personal network—and that really detracts from the fun and sense of community that a career journey could foster."

Are you ready to create your own career journey community? Let's get it!

ACTION:

Write down 10 more people you plan to reach out to and include their careers

Pull up generous

Suppose you meet someone today who changes your life forever. Now, imagine if you treated everyone you met with this possibility in mind.

This is a pretty exceptional and intentional way of approaching the way you connect with others. But it's true; no matter what you're doing, you are bound to meet significant and important people. It's key that you don't miss those opportunities.

"Start out every day with the realization that someone you meet today just might have a profound impact on the rest of your life," said Dan Casetta, a transformational leader with 30 years of experience at Vector Marketing/Cutco. "And if you start with that realization at the beginning of the day, you're going to be at your best that day; you're going to be looking for opportunities to connect, you're going to be opening conversations, and you're going to be making the effort to get to know people."

That may sound exhausting, especially if you're an introvert. And it does take added effort to show up every day prepared to make intentional connections. But I would like to encourage you to start in small ways. How can you get intentional with one or two social encounters today? Could you get more curious about the cashier at Trader Joes? How about the person sitting next to you at your local coffee shop?

When I'm at my fav coffee shops in San Diego (shout-out to Influx, Refill, Young Hickory, and Lestat's, you guys are the real MVP!), I like to take breaks from sending emails and working on *College Magazine* to connect with people around me. One of the easiest ways to do this is to get curious about what someone else is working on; this is especially easy in a coffee shop environment, where everyone around you is working on something interesting. I've met awesome people in a variety of fields this way—professors at local universities, entrepreneurs, professionals who work remotely, writers, and graduate students—a few of whom I've stayed in touch with and even a few I'm close friends with to this day.

Two professors I met invited me to speak on their campuses. One person I met, Nathan Young, invited me to speak at a local event, and later, I interviewed him on my podcast. I connected with another entrepreneur who I now meet with once per week for a group mastermind, where we offer one another expertise and feedback and keep each other accountable on our business goals. I've even ended up career coaching people I've met, connecting them with resources to grow their businesses and providing helpful introductions.

Next time you're out, before you check your DM's or slip in your ear buds, consider that the person sitting beside you on your flight could be your future mentor, employer, or friend. You'll never know if you don't take a moment to connect.

Dan takes a big-picture approach to his meaningful relationships. He thinks of it this way—you may not be able to see the impact of making these connections on a day-to-day basis, but if you meet just one world-changing person a year, imagine what that will mean for you 20 years from now. Your network will include 20 impactful people who may shift your mindset and inspire you in your life.

If you notice the endorsements on this book, you can see this mindset in action. I'm proud to have made dozens of important connections and to have met world-changing individuals over the years who have inspired me on my career journey.

These little moments of connection are also your practice rounds for the big leagues: real networking events, a.k.a. the often-dreaded, intentional, career-focused moments. So, make the most of it. Practice your handshake, your curiosity and three questions, and your passion elevator pitch (more on that in Chapter 9 where I cover how to speak your passion).

Living like this, every day you get to practice courageous connections. "I think it's important to be fascinated by people. To show a genuine interest in other people," said Dan. Remember, when you make a courageous connection, it's not about you. "Networking is about what you can do for others...what value you can give to others.

"Networking is about what you can do for others...what value you can give to others," said Dan.

Another way of thinking about this is "showing up generous"— a beautiful value statement that I heard from Jon Berghoff, co-founder of Xchange, as he kicked off the Best Year Ever Blueprint event. This message struck me. *Wow*, I thought, *if only every other conference and event began with this advice, perhaps we all would make even deeper connections.*

When you show up generous, you ask the people you meet how *you* can help *them*. This helps you learn the unique strengths that only you have to offer and also gives you an opportunity to fully understand the other person and their story. When I took Jon's advice at the Best Year Ever Blueprint, I learned that I was able to help a new friend with his public speaking. We both learned a lot about one another, and this sparked a meaningful friendship. This never would have happened if we hadn't embraced Jon's philosophy.

Jon started on an entrepreneurial path as a 17-year-old in high school working for Vector Marketing selling Cutco knives. He didn't love his traditional schooling, but when it came to sales, he loved the challenge. And while he didn't go to college, he was able to talk his way into getting an executive MBA at the Weatherhead School of Management because of his career experience alone. Yup, you read that right: talked his way in like a boss.

Today as the creator of the Xchange approach, Jon and his team design and facilitate interactions which produce incredible transformations for industry leading organizations. Jon has worked with some of the most prominent groups in the world including Facebook, BMW, TEDx, and Keller Williams.

"I feel like I get to wake up and live a dream," Jon said. "I feel honored that I get to do that."

Jon attributes his success to getting clear on what he values in life and who he aspires to be as a person. "Whatever we want more of in life, we need to give that," he said.

Think about that reciprocal concept for a moment. What do you want in life, and how can you give that to others?

Personally, I like to show up generous by offering my support, advice, and connections. For example, when someone tells me they're hoping to start a podcast, I offer to walk them through the process and review their introduction. I even connect them with people who have helped me on my journey and send them to my trusted audio editor.

At one of my speaking events, a student mentioned she wanted to work for the Peace Corps. I told her to follow up with me because my past editor in chief, Morgan, worked for the Peace Corps. I made the connection, and the student was able to set up an informational interview.

I revel in public speaking (I know I'm weird, don't judge me) and helping others with their presentations. I love showing up generous in this sense by providing feedback on business pitches or presentations since I've been there and know how stressful the process can be. It's an incredible feeling of pride to see three students go on to win a business competition after helping them refine their pitch.

Of course, I won't be helpful to everyone in every situation. Nor do I believe that we all have the time to give our help. But we can all try.

A couple examples of ways you can be generous include giving feedback on someone's project, making edits to a paper, helping someone with a complicated math problem, being there for someone to practice their presentation, offering connections you've made, or simply lending an ear to listen. It never hurts to ask someone how you can help. You may be surprised how much you'll make their day.

ACTION:

How do you show up generous and leverage your strengths to help others? Write it down.

Level up your network

Remember when I mentioned in Chapter 1 that you shouldn't just stumble into your career? Well, you don't want to stumble into your network, either. Don't simply rely on circumstance to place you in the right room at the right time with the right people. You need to get intentional when it comes to networking.

And the numbers don't lie—according to the research group Performance-Based Hiring Learning, 85% of all jobs are filled through networking.[19] Oh snap!

Christopher Lochhead, a former Silicon Valley chief marketing officer for three separate companies, strongly believes that who we surround ourselves with matters. "We become who we hang out with," Christopher said. "Be insanely thoughtful about who you surround yourself with." When we're intentional with our connections, we find people who will inspire and motivate us on our career journey and in life in general. And as Christopher points out, "legendary people hang out with other legendary people."

Are you ready to level up your network? Let's start with the most obvious networking opportunity: the career fair.

When I was in college, I felt lucky that I even remembered to *attend* the career fair.

Well, actually, my roommate mentioned the career fair the morning of the event and I thought, *Hmm, I should probs go to that.*

It was a crisp November day in 2007, the fall of my senior year at the University of Maryland, as I rushed over to the student union. I had printed off a few copies of a souped-up resume, which I luckily had ready to go from a recent English class assignment. Sporting my only professional outfit, a black pantsuit I bought for a presentation for the Quality Enhancement Systems and Teams (Quest) business honors program, I felt confident and ready to rock the career fair.

As soon as I stepped into the auditorium, that confidence fled. I immediately felt overwhelmed. I looked around in awe at the hordes of students in black and gray and navy blue. Anxiously browsing the company names printed in bold at the top of each booth, I hoped to recognize even just one brand—but to no avail.

After what felt like hours scanning the crowds, I finally saw a familiar face. It was Kate, a recent graduate from the Quest program. She was recruiting for her company, a government consulting firm. She had a queue of students waiting to talk to her, so I got in line.

When my turn came, I shook Kate's hand and mentioned how I remembered her from Quest. I could tell that she was excited to hear from a fellow Quest student; it was one of the highlights of her academic career. I shared that seeing her presentation at my first Quest informational session was what inspired me to join the program in the first place.

I told Kate how my first Quest team invented a top bunk bed storage system called "The Skyscraper." We held focus groups and designed prototypes until we had it just right where it could hold books, an alarm clock, and a clip-on lamp without toppling over. I could tell Kate was flattered that she had made such an impression on me. After catching up for a bit, I passed her my resume. Kate jotted down her email for me and insisted that I follow up. So, I did.

Even though she was impressed, I was still concerned that I only understood the classroom version of consulting. Despite these fears, I displayed confidence in my application and email exchanges with Kate. Just weeks after the career fair, I secured an interview. I took the interview seriously, researching and reading articles about the company to understand their purpose.

After talking to other students who were exploring consulting, I submitted applications to a handful of other companies like Accenture and Deloitte and snagged a few more interviews. At the end of the day, I received only one offer letter—and it was from Kate's company.

I can say with 100 percent confidence that I was definitely offered the job because of my intentional connection. I don't doubt it for a second. I felt I had a knack for interviewing, a natural ability to enthusiastically talk about my experience in the Quest program, but that clearly wasn't enough to get me an offer from the other firms. It was the combination of my research, my portrayal of confidence, and—most importantly—my connection with Kate that landed me the job.

I thanked my lucky stars that I saw Kate at the career fair and was able to make a genuine effort to connect with her. There I was, a college senior with an official offer letter in hand for a job that many college students were gunning for.

Like me, Andrea Stone secured her dream job at a career fair (yes, they have those for adults looking for new opportunities too). She researched each school beforehand to see which were specifically seeking a school counselor. Her approach made waves with the hiring schools; it turned out that most people would approach each table cold, asking blind questions like, "Do you need a second-grade teacher?" Andrea was able to stand out by knowing their needs ahead of time. Talk about a brilliant way to differentiate yourself.

Just like the time you spend researching someone before an informational interview, take the time to look through the company list at any career fair you'll be attending. This list is often easily obtained by either looking online or contacting the fair organizer or the career services coordinator. If you have that list ahead of time, you can map out your game plan, do your research, and impress the recruiters. Having a foundation of knowledge will differentiate you from others who are aimlessly wandering from table to table asking basic questions—this information is easily and quickly accessible.

This is the difference between attending a career fair intentionally versus attending on a whim. In today's competitive world, you must stand out, and your intentions are the perfect way to start. By demonstrating your genuine interest, you'll create a stronger connection with recruiters, which can spur deeper conversations about your experience to determine if you're a good candidate.

Since you've already made the commitment to attend, you might as well show up intentionally and treat every connection like it's going to be the one that will change your life.

I get it—career fairs are overwhelming. But, the 2 hours of your time plus the 30 minutes of upfront research is a small price to pay for direct access to a company of your dreams. Not to mention, you'll gain instant connections with potential mentors.

Keep in mind that not every career fair is going to lead you to your dream career. Your university career fair may only attract large firms seeking STEM majors, and if you're an art history major with a passion for museum and arts programs, you might need to find out where *these* organizations gather to hire. Not every industry hosts their own career fairs, but you may be surprised to find the ones that do.

Seek different event opportunities that fall within your field such as conferences, professional organization networking events, and social meetups. If you're passionate about museum and arts programs and you could see yourself in a marketing role, consider joining the American Marketing Association or simply attending one of their events.

Look to your local art museums and go to their after-hours shows and mixers. These aren't traditional venues for hiring, but they're excellent networking events that often lead to connections and employment conversations. In this case, you're not necessarily talking to a recruiter—so simply show up curious!

What I love about professional conferences and events is that you can learn about specific opportunities within companies who organize the events themselves. That way you're on the inside—you could be booking guest speakers and working with decision makers in your field.

When you start to connect intentionally, you start leveling up your life. Your bond with people who are aligned with your way of thinking will automatically be stronger than others. These are your people. This is your community.

"Attract the best; repel the rest," said Dr. Sean Stephenson.

Let me break that down for you. There are people in the world who don't care one bit about your passions—or theirs! They have accepted their fate and and will likely encourage you to do the same rather than go after your dreams.

This is why you need to put in overtime to find people who are like-minded; people who are reading this book, wanting to make a change, and ready to take action. You need a cheerleading squad. You need to level up your life.

Dan Casetta is passionate about helping entrepreneurs, leaders, and salespeople succeed and build meaningful relationships. He believes that most people are not committed to living their best lives. In fact, he feels that only about 10 percent of people are actually willing to strive to live the kind of life that you, by reading this book, are hoping to live. With so few of us focused on living an intentional life, you're going to face a big challenge meeting these people—especially if you're approaching your networking in a haphazard way.

But fear not! There's one surefire way to guarantee that you're only attending events with other 10-percenters: *pay money* to attend those events. "When you go to [an event where] people pay to go learn, they pay to go advance their own personal growth, almost all of them are in that 10 percent," Dan said. Think about this the next time you find yourself on an event registration page and notice that you're shocked by the price tag. I had a similar attitude until I started attending industry conferences, both for my own industry and for industries outside my bubble.

For example, I love sharing about my professional experiences at the Best Year Ever Blueprint. I felt inspired by every speaker that took the stage and was surrounded by the most positive and encouraging people I have ever met—all in one room. I was finally with a group of like-minded individuals; people who wanted to grow their businesses, make an impactful change in their lives and community, and learn from the best. These were people living with intention. People like me.

There are no guarantees that you'll meet people like this on an average day, so why not take that extra step to guarantee it by attending these events? *Hello?* Do your research, understand the goal of the event, and select ones that align with your passion and that will attract the community you want to be a part of.

Carey Smolensky, author of *Living Life with Passion and Helping Others,* is the executive producer of his own live event, The Passion Summit. This two-day immersive personal growth conference emphasizes making a difference in the lives of others. Carey's passion community focuses on supporting one another while thriving personally and helping others achieve their dreams. A big part of why Carey believes in the importance of his events is the way they help you level up your relationships.

Carey challenges himself every day to make a difference in the world. He believes that change is the key to innovation and he's constantly evolving, both personally and professionally, in order to live his life with passion. When you attend Carey's event, you are surrounded by like-minded people. That's when the magic happens.

Look up the career fairs, industry, or passion-related events you can attend in your city (or even travel to) that will level-up your network.

ACTION:

Investigate and list five events. Here are some examples of industry events you can attend:

- American Marketing Association
- Ignite
- Girls in Tech
- League of Women Voters
- Human Rights Campaign Gala
- MozCon
- ERE Recruiting Conference
- Print and ePublishing Conference
- BlogHer Conference
- Journalism Interactive
- IA Summit
- Converge SE
- Fashion Confidential
- Forbes Women's Summit
- SXSW
- Grace Hopper Celebration of Women in Computing
- TechCrunch Disrupt

If you're not sure of an event that's the right fit for you, hop on Eventbrite and Meetup and search your industry. From there, go to the event page and peep the reviews. You can even check out their Facebook pages and connect with past attendees to see if it seems like a good fit for you.

Every time I've attended a conference, I've made a connection (oftentimes more than one) that ends up impacting my career. For example, at Pubtelligence, a publisher conference, I connected with David Schmeltzle, founder and president of Bizbudding, who helped drastically improve College *Magazine*'s site speed and integrate the technology we needed to launch our online course, The Content Strategy Lab.

Pro Tip:

For entrepreneurs, it sometimes feels like you're on an island, coming up with ideas in isolation and motivating yourself to turn that vision into a reality. As someone who has done this, I can tell you that attending motivational events and joining learning communities are a game-changer. For example, Marie Forleo's B-school, Hal Elrod's Best Year Ever Blueprint event, and Carey Smolensky's The Passion Summit have all made powerful impacts on my life. I've met people just like me, and we often become each other's accountability partners. Accountability partners help keep you on track with your goals, and it's a comforting feeling to know that you are not a loner on your career journey.

Networking isn't exclusive to designated networking events. You can always set yourself up for networking moments by surrounding yourself with likeminded people. Another easy way to do this is by being on a college campus or taking a continued learning course that connects to your passion.

"Networking for me was less about going to events and handing out my card. It was just becoming friends with people…building a group of contacts and friends," said Will Hansen, the experience design manager and visual product lead at Intuit. In his visual arts courses, Will was constantly surrounded by other passionate graphic designers. In the process of making friends, he would try to learn from his classmates.

Amy Lisewski has a ton on her plate but, like Will, she's always looking to build a cohort of connections who share her values. She is the founder of Finest City Improv and the San Diego Improv Festival, and as a keynote speaker, Amy helps companies improve communication and collaborations using improv skills. She is also the author of *Relax, We're All Just Making This Stuff Up!: Using the tools of improvisation to cultivate more courage and joy in your life.* Before becoming a professional improviser, she ran an information and research consulting business, taught with Teach for America, and was a video and new media producer. Talk about a nonlinear career journey!

Despite her jam-packed schedule, Amy continues to surround herself with like-minded people. "Find your ensemble… Build trust and support with [each other]," she said. When meeting new people, Amy encourages you to uncover interesting things that person is doing, because this leads to more meaningful relationships and can build a solid foundation of trust.

By asking questions that dig a little deeper, people often share more. It makes sense: People love to talk about themselves. Would you be surprised to learn that on average, we spend 60 percent of our conversations talking about ourselves?[20] When you ask questions about someone's life—it allows them to talk about themselves (their favorite topic!)—and makes you more likable. According to research by

Harvard faculty, this isn't just conjecture; there is actually a consistent relationship between question-asking and likability. "People who ask more questions are better liked by their conversation partners."[21] When we ask more questions, we're perceived as better listeners who care.

When reflecting on her passion career journey, Amy shares that she has had three completely different careers—and her ability to make powerful connections in a myriad of spaces has been key in allowing her to move between industries.

"I don't think I've ever gotten a job just sending in a resume to somebody," she said. "I've always gotten it from knowing somebody, talking to people, building my know, trust, and like factor." Know, trust, and like happen when you build a relationship where you get to know one another, they trust you, and they like you. Not only will you feel more satisfied in leveling up your network, but it can help you take the next step of your career.

ACTION:

With your own passions in mind, clarify who may be missing from your circle. Then, use this to help facilitate new connections and aid in leveling up your network.

#SquadGoals

We talk a lot about mentoring, but what does it really mean? At its core, a mentorship is a relationship with a person in your field or with expertise that you can learn from. Your mentor can inspire you and lead you down the road of success. Believe it or not, one of the most vital connections you'll have in your career journey will be with your mentor—and after connecting courageously, holding informational interviews, attending events, and leveling up your network, you'll want to keep your eyes peeled so you can identify the right mentor for you.

I'm not saying that every connection or informational interview will result in a mentorship, nor should they—but some may. You can sniff out the probability by following up and seeing if the person you connected with is interested in offering feedback, giving more advice, or meeting up again in the future. They will either express interest or fizzle out. It's rather easy to tell when you're clicking, just like with any new friendship—except this friendship is sparked by a shared passion.

With a mentor, you share more than just a passion; you both want to see you succeed. You both enjoy talking about your path, and you're both looking to help achieve your goals. This might sound one-sided, but as someone who has acted as both a mentee and mentor, I feel so grateful as a mentee, but I also feel incredibly honored to be a mentor.

I've mentored fellow entrepreneurs, high school students, and peers who are jump-starting their own businesses. I adore talking shop and advising on how to stay focused on achieving goals. I also mentor college students and young professionals on creating intentional career journeys, especially *College Magazine* students and alumni. Witnessing their journey and seeing them succeed gives me such a sense of pride.

On my own career journey, I've had incredible mentors who I can't thank enough for advising me and helping me along the way. Keep in mind, I started *College Magazine* as a 22-year-old—what did I know about running a nationally syndicated publication and monetizing that business? Not enough. Most everything I learned stemmed from my mentors.

I've had plenty of people give me advice over the years, but one in particular stands out above the rest. From the moment I sold my first print magazine advertisement back in 2007 to the day I launched my first podcast episode in December 2018, Asher Epstein has been in my corner and with me every step of the way as my mentor.

I first met Asher when he was the managing director of the Dingman Center for Entrepreneurship at the University of Maryland. He spoke at my entrepreneurship class my senior year to explain how students could pitch their ideas, receive feedback, and even get connected with funding. Once my idea for *College Magazine* had won a class assignment, I felt that I had a business pitch worthy enough for the Dingman Center.

I had heard through the grapevine that Asher's feedback on pitches could be particularly harsh. I knew I needed to make a compelling case for the business. As a typical college student, I stayed up until the crack of dawn before the presentation with my friend, Chris Testa, beefing up the business plan. Chris later helped me launch *College Magazine* by building our first website and editorial workflow platform (where we shared documents and posted articles ready for edits), but that night we weren't just working on the nuts and bolts; we were prepping frantically for what we thought would be a tough battle.

The next day, we sat down at a conference room table and fearfully presented our plan to the Dingman Center's team. They didn't seem so scary after all—in fact, they actually looked impressed. I'll never forget telling Asher about the jobs Chris and I had lined up for post-graduation, mine at the government consulting firm and Chris's at Google. Asher flashed a big smile and laughed: Here we were, signed on for jobs other students were gunning for, and meanwhile trying to launch a startup company. There was no way we could do both once we graduated.

Even so, the Dingman team liked our idea and said that if we created a mockup of the magazine and sold a handful of advertisements to prove our concept—a minimal viable product (MVP)—they would be willing to invest up to $10,000.

Chris and I left the meeting completely elated. The Dingman Center loved our idea and wanted to invest in us with more money than we could have ever imagined. What an incredible feeling!

From there, without even thinking of it as a mentor-mentee relationship, I kept in touch with Asher. I shared our progress— when I sold my first ad, when I held our first photoshoot, and when we were finally ready to print the first issue.

Asher stuck by my side through it all, from that very first vision to today. I don't know how to fully thank him for believing in me, challenging me, and most of all, making time for me in his busy schedule. He's an ambitious individual who takes on some incredibly challenging projects. Today, he's the general manager of VIVA Creative, facilitating client events and business development projects. The fact that he has given his time to me and other young entrepreneurs speaks volumes of his generosity.

What I've learned through my relationship with Asher is that mentorship doesn't require organized structure. We were able to stay in touch after my graduation and even after Asher moved on to new opportunities following his own passions. A mentorship doesn't need a university or shared location to tie two people together; it simply boils down to the relationship between the mentor and mentee.

Any time I pivot my business, experience a significant challenge, or achieve a new milestone, I confide in Asher. I trust his feedback, but I also need his tough approach. I typically take an idealistic stance when it comes to my ideas, as my enthusiasm can lead me to take on too many new projects. Asher, thankfully, is a realist cheerleader. He isn't afraid to tell me when I've deviated from my scope, lost focus, or when one of my ideas lacks scalability. Yet, he's incredibly encouraging and reminds me of my strengths—especially my perseverance—anytime I start to feel twinges of doubt.

After that first pitch, Asher introduced me to Zoey Rawlins. Zoey was a recent University of Maryland MBA graduate who had founded a magazine called *SHOP DC*, which she eventually sold to Washington Post Media. I met with her in person, and what started out as an informational interview to learn more about her journey developed into another mentorship.

I looked up to Zoey because she had paved the way. She had transformed her vision into a reality. The quality of her beautiful, glossy print magazine was exactly what I was looking to create with *College Magazine*. I was in awe of her confidence to pitch and sell her business to none other than the iconic *Washington Post*. With Zoey, I felt understood; she knew what it was like to sell advertising, create a compelling magazine cover, tackle deadlines, and experience printing mistakes.

As our relationship grew, I had the chance to see Zoey evolve in her own career. After working as a manager in e-commerce and retail for the *Washington Post*, she went on to work in sales and business development for Groupon ahead of their IPO. Later, she was the national media director for WeddingWire and today she's a digital product manager at Capital One. Zoey's creativity and incredible ability to understand her audience has helped her grow in the field of product design and marketing.

When it came time to actually print my first issue of *College Magazine*, I reached out to another contact from my internship at *Washington Spaces* magazine: Angie Grandizio, the art director.

Angie oozed creativity, from the chic décor in her office with colorful fabric swatches, inspiration boards, and cover art lining her walls, to her trendy business professional style. I remember feeling nervous to approach her when I first started at *Washington Spaces*. She was always busy, and she was important. I had the chance to work alongside Angie near the end of my internship, helping her execute her vision during the photoshoot for my luxury doorknob article. We had a blast laying the hardware in beautifully designed layouts.

I still keep in touch with Angie to this day and consider her another one of my mentors.

I'll never forget the call I had with her after my internship when I pitched my idea for *College Magazine*. She was so impressed and supportive. Although we hadn't been particularly close during my time at *Washington Spaces*, Angie ended up sharing everything I could possibly ever need to know about entering this business, from advertising sales to the cost of printing.

I remember vividly that it was a beautiful day outside. I had plopped myself down on a bench outside my college apartment for the call; but after just 10 minutes on the phone with Angie for what I thought would be a casual chat, I found myself hunched over a journal taking detailed notes like a mad woman: 70-pound paper, signatures, bleeds. What the heck did this all mean?!

Listening to Angie talk was like hearing a new language, but luckily, she was fluent and more than happy to help translate. She explained brand-new concepts to me. I would have never guessed that magazines aimed for 60 percent of its pages to be advertising in order to be profitable. She suggested a couple printing houses to reach out to for quotes.

I worked around the clock. I was leaning on my mentors a lot, but I feel grateful to have had a team like Asher, Zoey, and Angie having my back. I can't thank them enough for being there for me.

And frankly, I don't think I *have* thanked them enough. I've always imagined thanking my mentors once I've crossed some ambiguous finish line, checked off that final monumental box, achieved an unintelligible amount of success. But what's more important is showing gratitude throughout the journey. It's not about hitting a goal. Goals are always shifting, anyway. Be thankful for all of the little things along the way; those small moments add up to incredible relationships.

When I think back to my mindset as a 22-year-old, I know I could have never anticipated owning and running a company today. I hope that Asher, Zoey and Angie know that their continuous support and advice along the way were invaluable in helping me pursue my passion. I am so grateful to have had them as my mentors.

I wish for you all to find your Asher, Zoey, and Angie. *#SquadGoals*

My point is, you don't have to embark on your career journey alone. And while your parents, family, and friends can offer a certain kind of support, those relationships are very different from an intentional mentorship. A mentor speaks your language and has the industry knowledge, connections, and experience to help you succeed.

Connecting with an adult or someone you look up to during your formative years really makes a difference. Knowing that someone believes in you will motivate you. It means the world when someone says: "You're qualified" or "You're on the right track" or "You're crushing it". We need these reminders, and I am fortunate to have had them. I want that for you, too.

Sometimes we get lucky. Someone sees something in us and makes the effort to stay in touch and build that mentoring relationship. More often, though, it takes thought and time to make a connection like that. Flexing this courageous connection muscle today will serve you every step of your journey. Sun's out, courageous connections guns out!

We need mentors at every stage in our lives, no matter how steady we feel in our careers. Even to this day, when I hop on a call with my mentor Asher, he reminds me to never give up and his words motivate me to keep going.

There's a mentor for every field and situation. I may have leaned on my mentors primarily for advice on running my business, but I also went to Asher for salary advice when I received my offer letter from the government consulting firm.

There are tons of ways you can ask for help. You can and should send your resume to a mentor for feedback. They may have advice for you when you're ready to advance or change your career. Your mentor can be someone to turn to when asking for a raise or promotion. In nearly every situation, they've been there and have the expertise to advise you on your next steps.

Take advantage of these moments where you feel inspired by others. Don't be afraid to ask someone to be your mentor. Connect courageously. Stay in touch. Grow the mentorship. And *always* remember to thank your mentors.

ACTION:

Who do you see as a mentor or potential mentor? Write down some names. Once you have your list, reach out to connect, ask questions, and learn from these mentors. Consider asking if you can send them your resume for feedback.

8

LAUNCH YOUR SWOOSH

Employers will Google you. Mentors will Google you. Coworkers will Google you. Do you know what shows up when someone searches your name?

Let's make the results shine bright like a diamond.

You've probably been told a million times to build your personal brand. What does that mean exactly? You're a person, not a brand, right? Well... personal branding is no longer reserved for the Instagram influencers or YouTubers of the world. It's for everyone. Your personal brand is a digital manifestation of your passion. It's where you can provide evidence of all your hard work.

Full disclosure: I didn't have anything close to resembling a personal brand when I graduated from college in 2007. Although the term was coined by Tom Peters back in 1997, I didn't even hear those two words spoken together until much later in my professional life. Nowadays, with the advancement of technology allowing endless opportunities to differentiate yourself online, the concept has been drilled into all of us. We've even dedicated an entire content vertical to it in *College*

Magazine to show students how they can build their personal brand while still in school.

According to Tom Peters, in his article in *Fast Company*, "The brand is a promise of the value you'll receive."[22] Sounds pretty important, right? You want to share your value with potential employers.

Fast forward to 2019: I won't pretend that my personal brand online today is *that* impressive, or nearly up to my own standards. But it exists, and it takes many forms that connect to my goal—helping young professionals create an intentional career—in the form of a LinkedIn page, personal branded website, podcast, and, *duh*, this book! Again, my personal brand isn't yet everything I hope and dream for, but, just like everything else in the career experience, it's a journey. Needless to say, we can't build our personal brands overnight.

So, now's the time to turn your passion and intentional experiences into physical representations of who you are and what you want. Your personal brand can be established through a LinkedIn profile, website, social media channel, or digital portfolio. You'll want to choose the social platforms and tools that align with your interests and your potential field.

Pro Tip:

If you have zero digital footprint right now, start off with an easy baby step: create a LinkedIn profile and add your photo, educational background, and one or two intentional experiences or jobs. If you're feeling a little extra motivated and inspired, look into buying your domain name. That's right, your name as a URL—think "www.amandanachman. com". Even if you don't use it right away, you never know when it might come in handy.

When creating your personal brand, a good stepping-stone is forming your resume. Your resume is a great starting point for taking all your intentional experiences and fleshing them out in writing. That way, you can pull from your resume to showcase all of these experiences on any personal branding platform. Your passion will determine which platform is right for you.

What do I mean by platforms? I mean any of the following:

- LinkedIn
- Personal branded website (www.you.com)
- YouTube channel
- Photography portfolio on Wix or Squarespace
- Vimeo account
- Facebook page
- Instagram
- Shopify or Etsy store

If you already have a resume, that's awesome! You're ahead of the game. Check the tips below to see if you can fine-tune what you already have. Hint: even the best resume can be tweaked. And if you haven't written yours yet—it's time to get started!

Write a kickass resume

It's true what they say— recruiters know in six seconds or less if your resume belongs in the "yes" pile or the "no" pile.

As an idealistic and naïve 21-year-old, I never believed my professors when they'd warn of this. As a professional, 13 years wiser, I've reviewed more than a thousand applicants' resumes, and I know there isn't enough time in the day to fully read (or even skim) every resume in the first round of screening.

Even if recruiters had the time to fully ponder every bullet point on the page, your resume is still not meant to be a long enjoyable read; it's a snapshot that tells your most impressive highlights.

You need to make sure that six-second glance makes a positive impression, especially with the one part you can control the most: the *quality* of your resume. This means the aesthetics, your word choice, and substance.

Let's get started!

Place the most important intentional experiences at the top, including your education, especially if you've graduated within the last 10 years. You've invested in yourself by working toward a degree and you don't want to bury this fact at the bottom of your resume. According to our *College Magazine* interview with Millie Robinson, Human Resources (HR) consultant and former HR director at *The Village Voice*, "At this point, your $150,000+ education may be the most important thing you have going for you. Pump it up! Add the city and state of the university."

If you didn't go to college, skip this part and instead, kick off with your real-life career experience.

You don't need to have all the experience in the world to start your resume. Just start with what you do have. Remember that your experiences are more transferrable than you think, so look back at the stories you wrote down earlier in Chapter 3 and use these to demonstrate your passion.

In terms of formatting, there are a lot of dos and don'ts for resumes. There are resume tips for every industry. Generally speaking, the simpler the formatting, the better, unless you're in a creative design field and you have the skills to build something impressive and clear. Keep everything on one page, and don't forget to include these basic key elements:

I. FULL NAME

Street Address • City, State Zip
Phone number • Email

II. EDUCATION

University Name, City, State
Bachelor of _____ expected _____or completed_____
Major: _____; GPA: _____
List honors and dean's list here

III. EXPERIENCE

Company Name, City, State, *Dates*
Your Position
- Description 1
- Description 2
- Description 3

Company Name, City, State, *Dates*
Your Position
- Description 1
- Description 2
- Description 3

IV. ORGANIZATIONS

Organization Name, City, State, *Dates*
Your Position/Role
- Description 1
- Description 2

Organization Name, City, State, *Dates*
Your Position/Role

- Description 1
- Description 2

V. SKILLS

List of skills with commas in between.

VI. INTERESTS

List of hobbies with commas in between.

RESUME BREAKDOWN

I. NAME

Start with your name, address, phone number, and email address. Increase the font size of your name (Between 14pt to 20pt) so it stands out on the page. I recommend simple Times New Roman, Cambria, Helvetica, or Arial fonts—the reliable classics. Comic Sans will get you shunned.

II. EDUCATION

If you're a recent graduate, list your college education first. Include your university's name, expected graduation date or your graduation year, major, and GPA.

Pro Tip:

Use whichever GPA is higher between your overall GPA and your major GPA. If your overall GPA isn't anything to write home about, consider listing your GPA for only the classes in your major, because often those grades tend to be higher than your overall average and are more applicable to your future, anyway. If both are under a 3.0, you may want to leave your GPA off.

III. EXPERIENCE

Next, feature internships, jobs, or leadership experiences. Below each position, list two to three bullet points on the important work you performed. If possible, include quantifiable information such as the number of events you planned, the number of people you led, or the number of dollars you raised. And describe your work using strong action verbs such as "led," "managed," "created," "organized" or "launched."

Passive: "I was on the swim team fundraising committee and got to make fliers to promote the event."

Active: "Created fliers to promote our swim team event as a member of the fundraising committee."

The list should be in chronological order unless you have experience that is incredibly relevant—but not the most recent—that you'd like to feature at the top. Make sure to use past tense unless it's a position that you currently hold and write in the first person, just excluding pronouns. Example labels for this section could be Professional Experience, Work Experience, Related Experience, or Employment History.

— Pro Tip: —

Exceptional resumes are stacked with numbers. In other words, they tell a quantifiable and specific story of your experience and they show evidence every step of the way. Look to where you can include numbers in each of your experiences: how many days of the week you interned, how many patients you interacted with, or how many readers viewed your article.

IV. ORGANIZATIONS

Include organizations you're involved in and be sure to highlight your leadership roles and responsibilities within that organization. This section is an opportunity to list your involvement with any clubs, nonprofits, sports teams, the Student Government Association, a fraternity or sorority, and/or volunteer work. Also add details on how you contributed to that organization's mission. Stay focused on your involvement during or after your college career. If you don't have enough material, you may include one or two significant experiences from high school. Label this section one of the following: Organizations, Community Involvement, Activities, or Campus Involvement.

V. SKILLS & MORE

At the end of your resume, list the specific skills that set you apart from the competition. Can you speak French, Mandarin, and Spanish? Or how about C++? Do you know how to use InDesign or Photoshop? These are impressive skills—brag about them. If you've been published, list the publications and include the article title. You can also use this section to share your hobbies: surfing, yoga, traveling, playing the saxophone, etc. Listing activities you're passionate about adds color to your resume and gives an employer another way to connect with you—who knows, your employer may love surfing too. Choose from any of these labels: Skills, Interests, Publications, Additional Skills and Interests, Passions, Languages.

If you're not feeling yourself today, stop writing your resume right now. Seriously: Go for a run, watch *The Office*, or cook yourself a gourmet meal. When you feel ready to cue your self-love, then, and only then, should you write your resume. Why? Because you can't write an exceptional resume if you aren't feeling exceptional. You are qualified, and this is your time to brag, brag, brag. Don't hold back. Take all the credit for your hard work and achievements up to this point. Show off and don't feel guilty about it even for a second.

Once your resume is written, go back in and spice up the language to be action-packed. That means replacing all the boring verbs like "was," "is," "have been," and "worked on" with action-verbs like "lead," "organized," "contributed to," and "created." Action verbs paint a picture of what you were actually doing in each experience. Think of your life like a movie—what do I see you doing in the scene when the director calls "ACTION!"?

Here are my favorite go-to action verbs for my own resume. Whenever I give resume advice, these are some of the most commonly used. See your resume jump off the page into motion when you inject these verbs into each description:

- Achieved
- Analyzed
- Built
- Created
- Communicated

- Contributed
- Demonstrated
- Evaluated
- Elevated
- Facilitated

- Generated
- Grew
- Headed
- Helped
- Identified
- Improved
- Inspired
- Interviewed
- Learned
- Launched
- Maintained
- Negotiated
- Orchestrated
- Organized
- Oversaw
- Performed
- Planned
- Produced
- Researched
- Secured
- Solved
- Spearheaded
- Supported
- Synthesized
- Taught
- Trained
- Utilized
- Wrote

I can't tell you how many people strike out at the resume stage because they don't take the time to put themselves in the shoes of the reader. The reader doesn't know what it's like to be you. They don't know what you did at your previous job. They don't understand how you spent the entire summer leading a group of 13 twelve-year-old campers at an overnight camp, developing their leadership and interpersonal skills. And they certainly won't get the right picture if you don't depict it properly.

It's fine to have your one-size-fits all resume, but you can go the extra mile by catering your resume to individual opportunities. In fact, you can even pull specific words used in a job posting and mention them within your own resume. For example, if the posting uses the action verbs "coordinate," "delegate," and "train," incorporate them into your resume. Don't forget, your resume is a living document that will change over time and can be adjusted for every single job application.

Once you have your resume, it's time to share it with the world. Your resume is not a secret, and the more you share it the more you can connect to your desired career.

Cue LinkedIn.

David Oates is an Accredited Public Relations (APR) specialist and a crisis public relations expert with 25 years of experience in the field. He helps organizations repair their brand's reputation in the press and online. He also happens to be the president-elect of San Diego Rotary and an adjunct professor at San Diego State University. Developing and protecting personal brands for his clients plays a huge role in his PR work.

When it comes to building your personal brand, David encourages you to look within, just as we did with unlocking your passion. "For starters, figure out how you want people to perceive you," he said. "That will come from looking at your core values, and then acting accordingly."

In other words, don't just build a brand that you think others want to see. "Build a brand that resembles you and then adhere to it," said David.

He's also a big proponent of communicating your personal brand via LinkedIn. "Since employers and recruiters utilize [LinkedIn] to seek prospects, I'd recommend optimizing it first before spending time to develop your own web page," said David.

Create an account today—yes, today. It should take no more than five minutes. For your profile photo, choose an image of you that's as professional as possible. So, skip those spring break selfies. This doesn't mean your photo has to be taken by a professional photographer or feature you wearing a blazer; just make sure that we can tell it's you, with a clear image of your face (no sunglasses here!). LinkedIn is meant for professionals to connect, and you want to put your best image forward.

Five minutes later, *voila!* You are Google-able.

Break the internet

If you want to share your resume in a more personalized fashion, consider launching your own website.

If you decide that a personal website makes sense for your passion, I am so excited for you. Anyone can easily create a personally branded site—even if it's for the sole purpose of showcasing your bio and resume. No tech background necessary, I promise!

A personal website provides online real estate you can use for any purpose or project imaginable as you continue to grow in your career. It's a place where you can decide at any moment that you want to blog, launch a knowledge-based course (ready to share your expertise on mindful watercolor painting?), or showcase your accomplishments.

I especially recommend personal websites for writers, because you can easily publish original pieces (no cold pitching here) and link to other sites where you've been published. Especially if you're a journalist, you want to continue to build and showcase your portfolio.

You can create a website in an hour without a background in web development. The final result is a place where your personal brand lives on indefinitely. Not bad for just one hour of your time!

Here are examples of other reasons to launch your own site:

- You have a portfolio of work to share:
  - Articles
  - Poems
  - Screenplays
  - Artwork
  - Videos
  - Photography

- You want to sell or link to something you've created:
  - Merchandise
  - Artwork
  - Knowledge-based courses
  - An expansion of an Etsy or Shopify store

- You want to link to sites that mention you:
  - Awards you've won
  - Articles you've written
  - Videos you're featured in
  - Articles written about you
  - Announcements that feature you
  - Pages online that feature you

- You want to blog daily, weekly, or monthly:
  - Share about your life
  - Blog on a topic
  - Share your passion (photos, travel adventures, favorite recipes, etc.)

Even if you decide to launch a store website such as Etsy or Shopify, it never hurts to also initiate your own personal branded website. That way you can link it to your shop while also having unlimited opportunities to grow your website (and business, too). You don't want to be limited by a second party site.

Will Hansen started his graphic design and photography portfolio site while still in art school. He decided to call it 3earedrabbit.com, inspired by the time he saw a three-eared rabbit.

Today, the image of a three-eared rabbit has become so much a part of his life that he even has a rabbit tattooed on his arm to serve as a constant reminder to follow his passion for creativity. How's that for personal branding?

"I wanted it to be unique, I wanted it to stand out from a crowd, and be okay with being a little bit different. That's what the rabbit means to me," said Will.

Will's site began as a portfolio site for his graphic design work. Throughout his career journey it has evolved to focus on his latest passion for photography (with an emphasis on people, travel, and neon signs). It features his photography, biography, a contact form, and a shop that connects to his artwork on Curioos, a site that provides graphic artists a space to sell gallery-quality prints.

This is the perfect example of having a personal branding site and a storefront site that coexist. Will can feature his skills and background as a design manager at Intuit while also showcasing his side passion for photography. Imagine how your personal branded site can be there for you as a place to share your work, especially as your passions evolve over time.

Eva Gardner began her professional career as a bassist immediately after graduating from UCLA with a bachelor's degree in ethnomusicology. In the time since, she has performed and toured the world with artists like Pink, Cher, Gwen Stefani, The Mars Volta, Tegan & Sara, Moby, and Veruca Salt.

Her personal branded website, evagardner.com, beautifully reflects her passions while remaining minimalistic and low maintenance. The page features a link to her Instagram where she shares more day-to-day updates and details, almost like a mini blog. This approach works perfectly when you want to communicate information directly without having your viewer get lost in a crowded site design.

If you're not a graphic designer and you don't want to spend a lot of time creating and maintaining your site, stick to the basics like Eva. On her website, Eva features her biography, favorite gear, press (articles, interviews, and podcasts), her music tracks embedded from SoundCloud, and her art portfolio (showcasing her other passion for visual arts—painting, photography, photo cards, and more).

Eva's site also includes a very straightforward contact form. This form is key for any personal branded site because it turns the website into an interactive communication tool. Now the site has exponential potential because you can grow your connections. Instead of always seeking opportunities, imagine if opportunities started to come to you through your very own contact form. How cool? Look who's in the power seat now.

How can you get started on creating your own basic (but growable) personal website to set the stage for future big announcements (ahem, like your first single release), like Eva's? It starts with a simple bio and a photo.

When you share your passion through a tangible portfolio, opportunities are bound to come your way.

ACTION:

Write down a few projects you want to showcase. What are you proud of?

Are you ready to take those ideas and create your very first personal branded website? Let's walk through it together.

Step 1: Buy your name.com

A domain is the URL, it's the address where your website will live. Go to GoDaddy or HostGator.

Type in your name.com and invest in yourself. For example: AmandaNachman.com. If your full name is taken, consider adding your middle name or first initial plus your last name. Most URLs are only about $12 per year. That's just $1 a month to own your name online. Vital and won't break the bank.

Step 2: Get your theme on

Some website builders offer you themes (the basic layout and design of your site) and hosting all in one package. There are advantages to some over others.

I'm a big fan of Mai Solution from BizBudding Inc. because it's the theme and hosting that I use for CollegeMagazine.com, College-Vested.com, FindYourPassionCareer.com, AmandaNachman.com, and 50by2050Project.org. Full disclosure, I'm an affiliate of the theme. I only put my name behind tools I trust. You can find a full list of personal branding tools that I recommend at AmandaNachman.com/resources.

The advantage to Mai Solution is that it's both exceptionally fast and reasonably priced, while also leveraging the WordPress Content Management System (CMS). If you're not familiar with WordPress, it offers non-techies a box called a WYSIWYG (What You See Is What You Get), which shows how the text you are writing (also known as copy) will display once you hit the "publish" button. The tool does not require any coding knowledge at all but can incorporate html if you want to get fancy with it.

Another advantage to the WordPress CMS is that it's highly valued by search engines like Google for its optimal SEO (Search Engine Optimization) tools. In fact, for these reasons it's used by Fortune 500 companies and massive content machines like Forbes, CNN, the New York Times, and TechCrunch. If SEO sounds like a totally foreign language to you, have no fear, just know that this tool allows you to become even more Google-able.

WordPress themes provide the skeleton for your site; without these bones, you'd need to code it yourself. Once you have your theme, you can grow the website as big as you want and become more discoverable online. I highly encourage this type of site for anyone who enjoys blogging.

Step 3: Write a snippet about you

Once you've selected your theme, you're ready to create your first page. All you need is a brief paragraph about you—yes, you! This is your personal branded platform and when a potential employer gets there, they will want a glimpse of you speaking (well, technically writing) your passion.

All we need is one paragraph here—short and sweet. Share your passion and tell the story of you.

Step 4: Sweeten the deal with a closeup

Go through your Facebook, Instagram, or elsewhere and choose a professional photo of yourself in appropriate attire. Aim for business casual at a minimum. If you don't have a professional photo, ask a friend to take one. If you're looking for quality and don't mind paying a small fee, head over to Upwork, Craigslist, or even your alumni Facebook group and create a post asking for help from a professional photographer with a photo shoot. This doesn't need to be a cover photo headshot, or a glamour shot by Deb, it just needs to represent you in a positive way. After all, there's nothing like a professional photo shoot to boost your confidence.

Step 5: Get in formation

Now you can start to stylize your site a bit. With Mai Solution and similar platforms, you can choose a template for your homepage to break it up into sections. Don't worry right now about populating your site with tons of content and media. Your "about me" paragraph and photo are perfect to start. By stylizing and adding sections, you're simply reserving spaces for future content and plans for your site.

Step 6: Include your resume deets

Time to pull from that shiny-new resume. You can add a PDF of your resume or design a page with your resume details laid out. A creative approach could be to design a timeline with content from your resume that uncovers each experience with images (organization logos, images of your work, or photos of you at related events) as the user scrolls through the site—kind of like a fancier version of LinkedIn that will make any employer swoon.

Step 7 (optional): Release your blog

Map out a vision for your blog. Similar to your passion career vision, any project, including your blog, should have a distinct purpose and goal. What's the overarching idea for what you'd like to write about on a regular basis? The blog could be about your career journey—your personal experiences (stories straight from your resume or from the stories that you connected to your strengths earlier on in Chapter 3), different companies that you've researched, or people you've met and how they've achieved their current position. The blog could feature your thoughts on your field or life experiences that demonstrate your passion.

Pro Tip:

Plan before you write. Could you imagine how stressful life would be if my team and I had to start off every day asking, "What should we write today on *College Magazine*?" Ongoing content projects require content planning—or you might pull your hair out. Creating and continuing a blog shows that you're proactive and have the ability to plan ahead, a rare and valued skill set in just about every career.

For content planning, I love the free tool Trello. It allows you to map out your entire editorial calendar or interview guest list (like the expert sources that you'll interview on your blog). I'm also a big fan of bulk activity, which is when you set aside a large clump of time to get a lot done at once. Planning content this way allows you to get into the zone and really grind out your work.

When you're content planning, you're able to spend quality time mapping out what you want to write or produce. Instead of having to think up something new every day, the content or the idea is already there waiting for you.

First, create a brainstorm content map, like a spider web (central idea in the middle, with other ideas jutting out like legs), and brain dump anything and everything you could possibly even think about related to your subject. These ideas become blog topics. Take these and organize and expand upon them in your editorial calendar board.

Step 8 (optional): Draft your first blog post

You have your platform. You have your blog topics. Now, don't over-think it. Simply put pen to paper and write about a topic related to your passion field, yourself, or your career experiences (like an informal cover letter). For example, you can write about why you've started your personal site. The more often you write, the more you grow as a writer, communicator, and expert in your passion industry. Not to mention, the easier it becomes to *keep* writing.

If you're not interested in the work or time commitment of a personal branded website, you can leverage other digital platforms that will help you establish your personal brand in just minutes. There are platforms galore for building your personal brand online—from social media networks like Facebook (either with pages or launching a group page/community) and Instagram, to review sites like Yelp, or shop pages like Shopify—there are plenty of options that you can tailor to your specific field.

Get your hands on some b cards

In today's digital age, the concept of the business card is controversial and might seem "old school." That doesn't mean they're dead, though. If anything, a networking environment less saturated by business cards means a greater opportunity to stand out with yours. So, harness some #ThrowbackThursday energy and get yourself a stack of business cards.

I can't tell you how many networking and career-related events I attend where people are thoroughly impressed when I hand them a business card. Even just the act of handing one out makes an impression these days. It's truly shocking how many people just assume that digital connections have replaced the business card. But how many people do you actually follow up with after following their Instagram or LinkedIn pages? Probably not enough.

On a more practical level, business cards provide a quick and easy way to share your contact information. If you're anything like me, you don't appreciate others using their phones while interacting with you in person, as it harms the authenticity of the interaction. If you find yourself wanting to exchange information with someone but don't have a business card, you'll have to turn to your phone— or the most old-school, but least suave option of all: pen and paper (or crumpled receipt).

When someone hands me a business card, they stay on my radar. I keep their card on my desk, and sometimes it even haunts me (in a good way) until I follow up. It's a physical item that takes up space and is a physical reminder.

A business card speaks volume to your character. It says you're prepared, you're ready to connect, and you plan to stay in touch.

Ready to make a stellar first impression? I recommend hopping on VistaPrint.com for fast and super affordable business card options. Simply add your name, phone number, and email to any design of your choosing. The company even offers 250 free business cards to their new customers. It's that easy.

It will take no more than 20 minutes to do this, and you will feel like a million bucks the next time you meet someone and have a card to hand them. Do it with confidence, because you are a boss.

> *Pro Tip:*
>
> Choose a colorful background for your card. According to Adobe.com, colored cards can last 10 times longer than the standard white card. Why not make that first impression last?

Pump up your IG

Let's say you're passionate about yoga, meditation, and mindfulness. You desire to work for a wellness organization. Consider curating an entire Instagram feed dedicated to this passion.

For example, you could include a daily video of a new yoga pose, or feature an inspiring quote relating to mindfulness. You might read articles by experts and each week share what you've learned in a post and photo that reflects your learning.

Not sure where to get these images? Pull from your own life. Check out Unsplash for free-for-use photos. You can even design an image on a free tool like Canva—a tool I absolutely love for designing quote tiles to feature on my personal branded Instagram. Each week I pull my favorite quote from one of the people I interview on my podcast, like this one from Laurence Jackson: "There are going to be many challenges that come your way and there is going to be a lot of nay-sayers and a lot of doubt, and none of those things are bad. In some ways it just means you are on the right path."

It takes less than five minutes to make a graphic for a quote like this, and the result is a beautiful image that I can share to spread the message and inspire others.

This also serves as an excellent promotional tool for my podcast. I make sure to tag the person I quote so that they can see themselves featured and help spread the word to friends and followers to listen in.

Your posts don't have to be professional or perfect. As many personal brand experts will tell you, brands constantly evolve. In September 2018, Dunkin' Donuts dropped the "Donuts" from their name. That doesn't mean they won't be selling doughnuts anymore, but they've embarked on a new opportunity to grow in the custom coffee industry. Uber is constantly improving their app icon design. And did you know that Pepsi used to be named "Brad's Drink"?! Your personal brand will grow as your tastes evolve and as your industry changes. No one expects a young professional or beginner in the field to know everything, so be open to change.

Remember—no one expects perfection. Remember Marty and his MVP? Perfection is the enemy of getting it done. It's better to start building your brand today and worry about making it the best later. The biggest step is just getting it started.

It takes a lot of courage to put something out there, especially in the world of social media where some people receive thousands of likes and your fledgling account may not be super popular right away. When it comes to a professional career journey, everyone has to start somewhere. While it may be impressive to a yoga studio if your yoga Instagram page has a ton of followers, there are still plenty of studios that would be equally as interested in a passionate new teacher who is still creating their Insta page and keeps at it. At the end of the day, they will see your passion, and your passion shouldn't be swayed by "likes." Truly passionate people do what they love whether other people take notice or not.

Leveraging an established social media platform allows you to build a tangible, physically viewable case for your passion. It's the reason why we are so impressed by influencers, creators, authors, and speakers; they've turned their message into a deliverable product. Creating the account is the easy part, it's not always as simple to put yourself out there and actually *post*. It's bold. It's hard. But bold action makes all the difference.

Maybe you're shy and don't feel comfortable sharing your personal life. That's totally fine! Personal brands don't necessarily require that you reveal intimate details about your life. In fact, sometimes it's smart to keep it professional. On my Instagram, I mainly feature my podcast guests and their quotes. This ties back to my purpose and vision for my personal brand: to inspire others to follow their passions.

Perhaps you teach your friends yoga; you could ask them to submit a photo of themselves in their favorite pose. You might feature professionals in the field and talk to them about their messages.

Once you've defined your vision for your Instagram page, take advantage of the platform to connect (courageously, of course!). Instagram offers you the opportunity to follow related wellness organizations and connect with other yogis. Consider following five to ten yoga brands you admire and hashtags to stay on the pulse of the industry. Then search deeper for yoga studios and yoga influencers you've never heard of before.

One of the greatest features of Instagram is that you can easily message these individuals. Reach out and DM people one or two steps ahead of you in your desired career path (rather than someone like Shiva Rea, who might be one hundred steps ahead). Or if you *do* hope to connect with someone at the level of Shiva Rea, with 100,000+ followers, reach out through other methods where your message won't get lost in the crowd—attend her retreats, reach out to her media team, and fill out the contact form on her website.

Keep in mind that if a platform like Instagram makes these celebrities easily accessible, there will be even more competition in reaching them. And your message, while easy to send, can be just as easily ignored by the person on the other side. Don't give up just because you didn't hear back from one incredibly busy person. Try reaching out again and try connecting to people who may not be as inundated with messages.

Now that you've created a digital footprint for yourself that says, "I'm passionate about yoga, meditation, and mindfulness," it's time to use that platform. Through a quick Google search, I found a yoga company called Laughing Lotus. They have locations in New York, San Francisco, and New Orleans and offer yoga classes and retreats. They also have less than 50 employees, which means they're most likely a 99-percent brand (and that's a good thing!).

On LinkedIn, I found two people that could be a potential mentor to a fledgling yogi: their financial officer and yoga instructor, and their creative director. Imagine reaching out to these two and starting a conversation about your mutual passion. Then imagine the impression you will make when you can share your Instagram page that demonstrates that passion. Fast forward to your interview for your dream career and your personal brand is your differentiator—especially if you're competing for a job against someone with the exact same resume, strengths, and skill set.

Build a foundation to demonstrate your passion today. Get on Instagram (or your preferred social media platform) now and sign up for a new account. That's all. Just create the account. That's step one.

Don't stress step two, but when you're ready, go ahead and create your first post! Once you've tackled those two hardest steps, you can sit down and content plan; that way you're not starting from square one every day with the question: "What should I post today?"

Pro Tip:

If you are not feeling motivated to create intentional social media pages, at the very least clean up your current social media presence. That means no drinking, no keg stands, no partying, no vulgarity, no nudity, no red solo cups. Employers may only spend six seconds glancing at your resume, but if they're considering you as a candidate, they'll look for you online, if only to ensure that there are no immediate red flags. If cleaning up your presence is too much work, switch your profiles to private.

Show off your videos

Let's say your passion is music. You play an instrument and produce your own tracks. You're interested in a career in music production and dream of working with stars like Beyoncé.

At an event at the University of San Diego, I once had a student raise his hand and share this exact vision. I loved it—dream big! I asked him if he had researched local music production companies and reached out to their teams for informational interviews. I could see him light up because there it was: a tangible next step up the mountain that he could easily visualize versus the cliff-jumping feeling of trying to reach that amorphous final destination.

Building intentional experiences around his passion, researching local companies, and connecting courageously will help this student on his journey toward his passion career. When it comes to building his personal brand, many great platforms already exist for the music industry—YouTube, Vimeo, even Facebook live.

If you've chosen video as your medium and have created an account on one of these platforms, awesome! I'm excited for you.

Before you can start growing your platform, first things first—you need a video. You've chosen video as your medium because it doesn't scare you, but it still takes guts to hit "record" that first time. After that, it gets easier.

For this first foray, keep it simple. Record yourself playing your instrument. Record a mix you made and set it to an image. Or record yourself talking about whatever it is that you are currently learning about in the music production world.

Let's say you're interning at a small music production company in your city; show us a day in your life. Walk us through the process. Explain the equipment and how it all comes together.

If you're passionate about music technology or pro audio, you could take inspiration from a publication like CNET and make videos where you geek out over the latest technology. You don't even need to make a major investment by buying the gadget; instead, go test it out at stores, your university, internship, or industry events like The NAMM Show and simply talk about your experiences.

Maybe you haven't yet taken any steps toward intentional experiences, but you know you're passionate about music. Start getting intentional today. Read articles and books about music production, then share what you learned in a video. Show us how you put your learning into action by creating your first track. Every day you'll get better and your viewers will be along for the ride. Meanwhile, you'll start to develop your personal brand. You'll stand apart from many other folks who dream about a career in music because you put in the effort to show your passion.

Now that you've created your first video, spruce it up with a thumbnail image (the first image that shows up and the one you can pin on YouTube to show for promotional efforts). Keep in mind there are free tools available, such as the free tool Canva, where they already have the YouTube dimensions and example template designs to choose from. No professional design skills needed here.

Remember, it's okay to be an amateur at building your personal brand. You *are* an amateur! Simply show up and put in the effort and you'll be well on your way. Start small, make it great, and then grow. That's my mantra for any new creation of mine.

You'll be surprised by how impressed other people will be by your free designed template and iPhone-filmed one–minute video talking about a new pro audio tool you've tried out. The fact that you put in the effort to do this courageous yet small act sets you apart from everyone else who is too afraid to put their passion out into the universe.

Personally, I've been incredibly impressed with the evolution of Thomas Frank's YouTube channel starting from day one. He's an author, YouTuber, and founder at College Info Geek. We met on a trip in San Francisco sponsored by Adobe for bloggers in the college space. Thomas is passionate about helping students succeed. His YouTube videos, which have attracted 1.9 million subscribers and 111 million views, share college hacks and research on topics such as studying techniques, time management, and improving habits. He's informative and incredibly entertaining to watch. I learn something new from every one of his videos. By creating value for his viewers he's also showing up as an expert and speaking his passion for productivity and achieving success through improving his behaviors.

It all started for Thomas with the simple act of writing a script and filming a video. He went from zero to 1.9 million subscribers starting in 2006, improving with every upload. If video as a medium speaks to you, too, know that you can do it. Ready, set, action!

Start podcasting stat

When you were brainstorming what form you want your passion platform to take, did a podcast come to mind? If so, you are a total go-getter! This is a growing platform, and I highly recommend jumping on it if you feel comfortable recording yourself speaking (or if you're prepared to get more comfortable with your voice). Not only is it a great way to demonstrate your passion, a podcast is also a great tool to interview people in your desired field.

At Apple's Worldwide Developers Conference in 2018, the company confirmed there were over 550,000 podcasts available on their platform.[23] And according to a *New York Times* article by Jaclyn Peiser, the number of people who have listened to at least one podcast in their lives increased by 20 million in 2019, and an additional 14 million people described themselves as weekly listeners when compared to 2018's figures.[24]

I believe anyone can start a podcast. Like uploading your videos to YouTube, creating a podcast is free and open to all. Keep in mind that iTunes does require a submission and approval process, but you can easily stream your podcast on Libsyn, Spotify, or other platforms that have little or no barrier to entry. Not to mention, there's very little overhead cost to get started. You can get started with virtually zero tools other than your smartphone. To make your passion project a little more of a high-quality affair, though, I'd suggest starting with these initial low-cost items:

- Microphone: I started with the Blue Snowball USB Microphone at around $50 and today I use the Blue Yeti USB Microphone, which runs around $90.

- Headphones: You can easily get away with using any pair that you already have, like your iPhone earbuds. I use Audio-Technica Headphones (around $150) because they help eliminate feedback.

- Online Recording Tool: Unless you're recording in person, you'll need an online tool that allows you to record, like Skype or Zoom. I like that Zoom allows for recording both audio tracks separately. The monthly subscription runs around $14.

- Host: You'll need a space to host your podcast before it can be streamed on iTunes and Spotify. I use Libsyn, which offers plans at $5 a month.

- Bonus: An Audio Editor: I'm all about production and sound quality and I knew that I did not have the audio experience to create the end product I wanted. I found a talented audio editor via Upwork to make seamless cuts for each podcast and adjust the audio (around $45 per podcast). He also helped me record my intro and outro.

You can edit your podcast using iMovie, which is free on Apple iPads or computers, or you can leave your podcast unedited and just go with it!

I can't tell you how many people I know who have told me they would love to start a podcast. Set yourself apart by making moves.

I promise you, if you set aside the time, you can make a podcast. It does not require a diploma, expertise, or experience. It only requires passion to fuel your creation.

Similar to video, podcasts range in format. Consider which of the formats works best for your goals:

- Interview or Q&A
- Conversational
- Educational
- Storytelling

The interview format is one of my favorites because it allows you to establish yourself as a thought leader while also providing a fantastic excuse for courageous connections.

Another advantage of creating a podcast is that you can use it to establish your personal brand across multiple platforms. In other words, you can repurpose the audio content into a blog through direct transcription or turning the podcast story into a more structured article. You can pull your favorite quotes or notes in bullet point format (known as the "Show Notes") for your branded website. Take those quotes and design them into graphics for your Instagram or Facebook.

The key takeaway here is repurpose, repurpose, repurpose. Ask yourself, how can this one interview provide helpful content in multiple formats?

For example, I conduct a single interview for my podcast that I also record as a video to add to my YouTube channel. Then I leverage the interview by writing an article for my blog, featuring a photo of my interview guest on Facebook, Instagram, and LinkedIn with my favorite quote, and finally, by creating a tile image of the quote for another piece of promotional content.

Don't feel like you need to do all of this at once. Start with the podcast interview, and once you're comfortable with that process, introduce additional versions that allow you to repurpose and expand your content. It's helpful to know that you can expand the impact of one interview to build your personal brand across multiple platforms.

I follow the interview format for my podcast *Find Your Passion Career*. Here's how you can get started on the interview-style path if it fits with your passion and will help your personal brand.

Step 1. Create the V.I.P list

The first step is to create a list of potential guests. Start with your personal network: friends, mentors, professors, bosses, coworkers, etc. Before I launched my podcast, I held a trial interview with my best friend Kari. Starting with your friends makes the whole experience far less stressful. And they're more forgiving when you need to adjust sound levels or start and restart again and again. I'll never forget the laugh fest and millions of first takes I had interviewing my friend Andrea Stone for episode six of my *Find Your Passion Career* podcast.

After you've made your list, spend about 20 minutes sending emails to your contacts asking for an interview. Here are a couple example emails you can use—but be sure to personalize your emails as much as possible:

```
Hi _____,

How are you? I would love to interview you
on my new (NAME) Podcast.

Your story is such an inspiration, and I know
that (DESCRIBE YOUR AUDIENCE) will benefit
from your advice.
```

Please let me know if you have some time for an interview this month. Looking forward to speaking!

Sincerely,
(YOU)

Hi _____,

I'd love to interview you on _____ for the (NAME) Podcast. My goal is to highlight (INSERT THEIR UNIQUE STORY OR DIFFERENTIATOR). Please let me know if you are interested in being on the Podcast and if you have some time in the coming weeks!

Thanks,
(YOU)

Step 2. After they accept, schedule a time

If you haven't heard back yet, be sure to follow up, the same way you would follow up with a contact on LinkedIn asking for an informational interview. But if they *do* reply and are interested in being interviewed, it's time to schedule!

Hi (NAME),

Thanks so much for saying yes to the podcast interview!

Please let me know what works best for you or if any of these dates and times fit your schedule for a (HOW LONG THE INTERVIEW WILL TAKE) interview:

Jan 28 @ 10 a.m., 11 a.m., 12 p.m., or 1 p.m. PT

Jan 29 @ 12 p.m., or 1 p.m. PT

Jan 30 @ 10 a.m., 11 a.m., 12 p.m., or 1 p.m. PT

Looking forward to the interview!

Cheers,
(YOU)

Step 3. Get curious & generate questions

I find that it's helpful to have a general idea of the questions you'd like to ask every guest and then modify them to fit each guest's unique story and strengths. During the interview, feel free to remain open to stray from your prepared questions, but it never hurts to have a starting point and structure to lean on in case you blank once the recording starts. Here are some general questions I like to ask on *Find Your Passion Career*:

- How did you get started on this path in college and after? What were the challenges?

- What career advice do you have for college students today?

- Describe a day in your life in your career.

- Tell me about the object you brought and how it reflects your passion. (If you tune into to my podcast, you'll notice I ask each person to bring an object to talk about.)

- How does your career align with your passion/interests and/ or your strengths?

Here's an example of a catered version for a high-tech serial entrepreneur:

- What did you imagine as your career path when you were in school?

- What was it like to start your first company at only 18 years old?

- Describe a day in your life as a podcaster, best-selling author, and advisor/investor to Silicon Valley startups?

- What was it like being part of a software company and getting acquired by HP?

- Tell me about the object you brought and how it reflects your passion.

- How would you say your careers align with your passion/ interests and/or your strengths?

- What career advice do you have for college students today?

Step 4. Send email with interview deets

Prepare your guest for what to expect during the interview. I also ask for a bio and photo beforehand to include in the podcast intro, article, and promotion. Below is a real example of an email I sent—and notice how at the end I ask for permission to include content in this very book because I'm already thinking ahead about how I can repurpose and share some of the helpful information learned in the podcast:

Hey Christian,

Awesome! We're looking forward to interviewing you on Find Your Passion Career podcast!

Here's a link to the podcast in the meantime: (LINK)

Important Interview Details:

- Here's the Zoom video link: (LINK)

- Having a mic is helpful for better quality audio but not required.

- Please bring one object that reflects your passion (does not need to be career related). No rules here; have fun with this one!

- Feel free to come to the interview with a coffee or beverage like we're having a virtual coffee date.

Example Questions

- What did you imagine your career path being during college and after?

- Describe a day in your life in your career today.

- Tell me about the object you brought and how it reflects your passion.

- How does your career align with your passion/interests and/or your strengths?

- What career advice do you have for college students today?

Please reply with the following:

- 2-3 sentence bio for me to include in the podcast description.

- A headshot or professional work photo to include on the website.

- Permission for me to include quotes from our interview in my upcoming book about finding your passion career.

Cheers,
Amanda

Step 5. Get on their calendar

This step is key. If it's not on both of your calendars, be prepared to get stood up.

Step 6. Hit record

Before I kick off the interview, I like to share my vision for the podcast and explain simple ground rules like keeping the conversation clean (iTunes makes you flag your podcast if it contains explicit content).

Once we hit record, I try to keep the podcast within 25 minutes. Afterwards I always thank my guests for their time.

Step 7. Write out cuts & send to audio engineer

Cut any restarts, stutters, extreme "ums," and especially total, utter mess-ups or tangents that could make your listeners tune out.

Step 8. Repurpose your audio into a blog

Once the podcast is squared away, I think about the heart of the episode. What message made the greatest impact on me? What stories were inspiring? I take those highlights and write a five-hundred-word article to feature on my blog. In the article I include a handful of quotes from the interview.

Each blog follows the same format where at the end I include a call to action (CTA). Here is the template I use as my CTA at the end of every podcast summary article:

After listening to (NAME)'s story (INSERT LESSON).

Subscribe and download my podcast interview with (NAME) here on iTunes! (LINK)

Once you're inspired by (NAME)'s story, we would love to read your review. Thanks so much!

Want more advice on how to follow your passion career? Follow host Amanda Nachman & Find Your Passion Career on Facebook & Instagram!

Write a blog post that teases your podcast as much as possible to get the reader excited to tune in!

Step 9. Add the post to your website

Here are the steps I follow to post and publish the article/show notes about the podcast.

1. Title: (PODCAST NAME) Podcast Ep __: GUEST'S NAME, GUEST'S COMPANY NAME

2. Paste article on text side to avoid formatting issues and add any additional media such as images or video.

3. Add featured image. Add alt text description (This tells the viewer what the image is in case the image does not show correctly. Alt text also helps with Search Engine Optimization so that the photo can show up in Google searches)

4. Add relevant categories and tags.

5. Add a meta description. (This is a brief call to action that describes the article like a sales pitch. Meta descriptions can show in search and social media posts. The Yoast plugin on WordPress allows you to add the meta description to your post.)

Step 10. Add your new episode to a podcast hosting platform and stream

When you log in to Libsyn (or another podcast hosting platform), you can upload your podcast audio file and then include your description. From there you can also include your description that will show on iTunes and other streaming platforms like Spotify.

Voila! You're ready to publish your podcast.

Once you've published, it's time to promote. The idea is to reach out directly to your passion community to share your hard work and connect. This is where you turn quotes into Instagram posts and send emails to your guests and any related organizations to help spread the word.

9

PASSION IS CONTAGIOUS, IN A GOOD WAY

We grow up speaking our passion to everyone we know. But somewhere along the way we let doubt seep in and take over. We invite our inner critic into our heart and soul. We critique ourselves, nonstop.

Before we know it, we've stopped speaking our passions, hopes, or dreams—and when we do, it doesn't flow as easily as it did before.

Why do we quiet ourselves? Perhaps we don't want to brag, we don't think we're qualified, or we don't feel like our dreams are possible.

It's time to quiet the critic within and speak your passion now. Otherwise, you'll silence yourself while expecting different results for your career journey.

You can't wait until the day you've achieved your passion and proven your success to start speaking out. This is a recipe for disaster. You may be waiting until you're 70 years old, and by then, you very well could have let your intentional career journey pass you by.

When you speak your passion, you start to believe it. Others will hear you and believe it, too, and doors will open.

When Sarah from TodayTix spoke her passion for film, people in the field pointed her in the direction of even more gigs and opportunities to get involved. Doors opened.

I've personally experienced this incredible phenomenon throughout my journey with *College Magazine*. Every time I've spoken my passion, doors have opened again and again.

It was the summer of my junior year of college. I was working at *Washington Spaces* magazine. There's something about working on a task that completely bores you (like researching doorknobs) that starts to ignite the imagination. I asked myself, *If I could write about something that actually interested me, what would that look like?* That's when I started to think about the idea of a magazine on college advice. I loved my college experience and felt that I had a lot of advice to offer.

But I was still afraid to voice this idea. I loved the idea and wasn't open to opinions that may have contradicted that the concept was anything but exceptional. I wanted to keep it under wraps, safe in my own mind and far away from any judgment that may feed self-doubt. But that summer, I started bringing up the concept in conversations with trusted friends. It didn't feel as scary to share the idea with them, my inner circle. What was my fear, exactly? Maybe inside I realized how much I loved the idea and was worried that it wouldn't take off or that I couldn't achieve it, afraid that the idea was bigger than me. *Who am I to try to make this magazine?*

To my surprise, the more I spoke about *College Magazine*, the more confident I felt, and the more helpful feedback I would receive. Meanwhile, I got better and better at explaining the idea. I did hear from naysayers with mixed reviews, but I relished the positive responses, especially from my friends (who were also, luckily, my target audience).

As someone who values honesty and constructive feedback as I grow as an entrepreneur, I've begun to realize just how powerful support and positive feedback can be. Positive reinforcement adds fuel to our motivation.

With a group of supporters in my corner, I decided to leverage my entrepreneurship class my senior year as the platform to test my *College Magazine* idea and receive additional feedback. I felt ready to speak my passion on a new level by presenting to classmates who didn't know me outside of school; they weren't friends who would feel obligated to give me praise or hold back criticism.

Our professor, Brent Goldfarb, assigned us a one-minute "elevator pitch" for a business concept with the goal of convincing our classmates to drop their ideas and join ours. This was pre-*Shark Tank,* but the assignment had a similar cut-throat vibe. Each student had to gather a team of three or more. If you couldn't win over at least two other classmates, it was a sign that your vision just wasn't strong enough.

I was thrilled to face the competition, especially considering the assignment offered a small slice of how real life works. You're either doing your own thing—creating a business—or you're contributing to someone else's vision. Of course, you can still be entrepreneurial while working on someone else' vision (this is called intrapreneurship, which is when an employee develops an innovative idea within a company), but for the purposes of the class, we were either the winning innovator or not.

And I wanted to be the winner. By this point I felt passionate and ecstatic about my idea for *College Magazine.* And it showed.

After my elevator pitch presentation, I convinced two students to drop their idea and join *College Magazine.* We created the first version of a business plan and presentation for the class. Together, we won the assignment and the grand prize—a $50 gift card...split between three people. The true award was the pride I felt, and the validation of the business plan.

Speaking my passion had attracted two people to join my project. But that was just a class assignment, right?

After the class and, later, my successful pitch at the Dingman Center, I felt ready to create the first mockup of *College Magazine*—but I would need a team of student writers to make it happen. This would be the real test of speaking my passion. I was no longer in the comfortable testing grounds of the classroom arena.

I designed a flyer and plastered it all around the student union and dorms for students to attend our first potential editorial meeting. I had no idea if it would work or if anyone would even show up. But between the flyers and me speaking my passion to everyone who would listen that week, around 15 students attended.

I couldn't believe it. I felt like I could burst with pride and excitement. Students actually wanted to write for *College Magazine*. They believed in the idea, like me, even though the magazine itself didn't even exist yet. We were off to a fantastic start!

We needed to keep this momentum. We had great attendance at the first meeting, but I needed to continue speaking my passion—not to friends or classmates but to students I had never met before, some of whom were probably more talented writers than I was.

What kept them engaged at those meetings? Me, sharing my passion for this idea in a way that inspired them to contribute. They felt excited to write for the magazine and felt confident in my ability to deliver on my promise to publish their hard work.

At the meeting we brainstormed article concepts, writing them on the white board in the student union room, and assigned each article to a writer.

I started to notice more and more that my passion for the project was contagious. The more I spoke my passion, the more people would pipe up with ways they might be able to contribute. Two of our top writers, Matthew and Maureen, volunteered to take on our first editor positions. My friend Rachel, who had a small speaking role in the upcoming movie *National Treasure 2*, which was filmed on the University of Maryland's campus, happily agreed to be our first cover girl and feature story. Others offered to act as our magazine photographers. Before I knew it, we were standing outside of the campus theatre in front of a beautiful brick wall, helping Rachel strike poses for our very first photo shoot.

It felt like everyone wanted in. How cool! Just like that, my spoken words were transforming into actions. The magazine was materializing before my eyes, all because I inspired others to come along on the journey.

Even as I write this book, I continue to speak my passion to everyone I meet. Some people move on with their lives after our conversations; others ask me where they can read *College Magazine*, how they can join our mailing list, or where they can download the podcast or buy my book.

The feeling is overwhelming. When you speak your passion to those who share it, they will want to get involved or support you. If you haven't experienced this before, that's okay; I am excited for you to have these moments as you start speaking your passion loud and proud.

Just the other evening, I met a couple at a restaurant in L.A. who were at the table next to mine. When they asked what I did for a living, I mentioned this book. Though the book had not yet materialized, I put my dream out into the universe.

I'm speaking my future in my present. I'm rehearsing so when the book is available, I'm ready with a honed pitch. I'm also gauging reactions and getting feedback along the way. A gut response on your ideas from others can be very helpful.

So far, the responses I've gotten to this book have been overwhelmingly positive:

"This book is so important."

"Young people need this message."

"I had no idea what I was doing in my career when I started out. I felt so lost."

Feedback like this continues to fuel me and helps me focus on what's most important in this book. I tried So. Many. Titles. on for size before landing on "#QUALIFIED." I promise you that my family and friends have heard dozens and have provided helpful feedback at every step.

You can elevate speaking your passion too by talking to a professor, mentor, or to people you meet networking. A great way to engage someone when speaking your passion is to ask for honest feedback. (But first make sure you are open to hearing it.)

Most people are going to be impressed that you are putting your dream out in the universe and are speaking confidently about your passion. They will want to root for you and give you advice to help you down the line.

Fair warning: Don't expect this from everyone. There are people out there who will want to protect you from dreaming big, or who will project their own insecurities on to others by crushing any career idea that's in the arts, is nonlinear, or doesn't ooze with dollar signs. Move on. You have bigger fish to fry.

Like your next step—speaking your passion at an interview.

Everything up to this point—especially building your personal brand—has contributed to the moment you speak your passion at an interview. The key is how your personal brand aligns with you and your passion.

David Oates, principal at PR Security Service and adjunct professor at San Diego State University, explained how your personal brand can help you to speak your passion with ease. "Truthfully, it comes naturally if the brand you possess stems from your values. Too often, people—young and old alike—try to align their brand persona to what they perceive people want to see. That never ends well for it doesn't come across authentic or relevant. If you can't speak your passion through your personal brand, then your brand doesn't align to your true self. Change that."

But let's not jump ahead here. You've connected courageously, built relationships, and started creating intentional experiences and you've begun growing your personal brand. Before you get the interview though, you need to apply for something—or ask for the job you don't realize is available.

Get ahead of the game

What? Apply before a position opens? Amanda, are you crazy?

I promise you that this is a real thing.

Now that you've expanded your network through intentional experiences and courageous connections, let everyone know that you are looking for a position. How?

Send out an email. Talk to them. Set up coffee dates. Let them know what you're looking for and what aligns with your passion. Share your vision for your intentional career journey. Speak about how you plan to use your passion to contribute to the organization and learn and grow in a way that aligns with your interests, strengths, and values.

When I've needed a job, I've reached out to my network and gotten one, time and time again.

So, Amanda, what you're saying is that if I am passionate about mentoring young people, especially underserved youth, I should start telling my contacts I'm looking?

Yes!

It's all about who you know (your courageous connections), and it's all about how you speak your passion.

Christian Feliciano is an instructor for the College Apps Academy at Reality Changers, a nonprofit in San Diego that serves over one thousand youth from disadvantaged backgrounds in Southern California every year, guided by the motto, "*College changes everything.*" He's passionate about helping students from underserved backgrounds in order to one day close the achievement gap.

"It's really about teaching these students that they can believe in themselves, that they can go to college," Christian says.

Christian speaks his passion every day. And it's how he found his way on his intentional career path.

Born and raised in Paradise Hills of Southeast San Diego, he was inspired by his high school physics teacher and planned to return to his community as a physics teacher himself. Along the way, he realized he didn't enjoy physics and instead chose to major in chemistry.

Meanwhile, he sought out mentoring opportunities to give back to his high school while pursuing his undergrad degree. This was his *ah-ha!* moment. "That's when I figured out, I wanted to help students succeed inside and outside the classroom," Christian said, "so I took the outside of the classroom approach."

After graduating from the University of California, San Diego with a Bachelor of Science in Chemistry, his transition from university to the career world took time, patience, and trust. He faced rejection from a dream job in student support services, lost only by a small margin.

"It was crushing," Christian said of receiving that painful rejection. "Especially since I thought that I'm putting my all into my passion career, that the things I would want would come to me fast… I had to realize it's going to come to you at the right time. But, of course, absorbing that in that moment, it hurt."

In times of doubt, he turned to his support system and his resume to remind him of his accomplishments.

"I have to trust the process and that if I am going to be in the right position, it is going to come to me at the right time," he said.

Through a student affairs fellowship at UCSD, Christian met his mentor Noel, who was also passionate about education. Both were from Paradise Hills and went to Morse High School, which contributed to their mentor-mentee relationship's foundation. Noel had previously worked at Reality Changers and shared his experiences with Christian. Christian had never heard of the program but was thrilled to learn that there might be an opportunity to work there one day. By sharing his career vision with Noel, he was able to get invaluable guidance and get his foot in the door at a great organization. Noel was even able to recommend Christian for a position at Reality Changers. Christian wouldn't even have known about this opportunity had he not made this connection and spoken his passion.

This is how the intentional career journey works. You speak your passion and, before you know it, someone you meet suggests an opportunity. Doors open.

Now an Academy instructor, Christian teaches high school students how to be successful college applicants. He gives advice and feedback on college essays and—most importantly—makes connections with students and instills in them the confidence that they can own their stories.

"At Reality Changers it's not always about how much I know; it's about how much I care for [my students]," he said.

If you want to live your dream like Christian, you can't wait around for a door to open. You must intentionally build your experiences, connect, and speak your passion. Christian did this and was able to get his foot in the door as a result. He shared his mentorship experiences and landed the interview. He used his connections and his immense passion for helping underserved students to secure his dream job.

Josh Axelrod also spoke his passion, which led him to a job he loves. At a graduate school career fair, he shared his passion for journalism with a recruiter who was so impressed with him that she reached out when a position opened up in reporting on veterans' issues for *The Military Times*. From there, Josh flourished, and he recently accepted a position as a digital sports producer at the *Pittsburgh Post-Gazette*—which aligns directly with his passions.

"For me it's really the act of writing…the physical act of [putting] all of my pieces for a story together like a puzzle to make them as good as they can possibly be—that's when I look down at the clock and look up later and…I've been writing for three hours," said Josh. "I always just tell people that I love journalism, and I'm okay with reporting, but it's really just the act of writing that gets me up in the morning."

Note, though, that Josh made a courageous connection with a recruiter at a career fair.

"Do not stick your nose up at career fairs. They can work," he said. "Dress nicely. Print out your resume. Schmooze like you've never schmoozed before. And some good stuff can happen. It has worked out for me shockingly well the more I think about it."

Because he spoke his passion at the career fair, Josh now works in a job he loves. He spent five years creating intentional experiences by working in and around journalism for websites and publications like the *Washington Examiner* and *Pittsburgh Post-Gazette*. He also writes as a freelancer (hello, side hustle!) to build on his passion for writing about pop culture. Check out his fansided.com article on *Crazy Ex-Girlfriend*, his favorite show.

Josh is a perfect example of someone able to recognize his strengths and speak his passion. He even spoke his passion at one of his first jobs in order to take on more of the projects that excited him most. He was a copy editor and producer with the *Washington Examiner*, and Josh convinced his boss to let him launch his own beat called "Pop Politics." How? By taking action and proving that he had an idea that was of value to the publication.

Even on his cover letter, Josh includes a sentence about this very strength, "[I always say] I am enterprising."

Speaking your passion continues throughout your career journey. Like Josh, it will help you advance after you're already *in* your dream job.

Macey Spensley is currently seeking career opportunities outside of job postings. She's passionate about helping others who have diabetes and wants to work for the Diabetes Foundation. She asked if she should send a cover letter to them, even though there weren't positions open currently. I gave her an enthusiastic "yes" because this action will help them keep her in mind when the timing is right.

Macey has been a camp counselor at a juvenile diabetes camp and has mentored youth for years. She also shared her story about living with diabetes for *College Magazine*. When there is an open position available, I am confident that Macey's cover letter will not be forgotten.

Who knows, maybe they have something available that isn't public yet, or an internship or volunteer opportunity that can help her get her foot in the door. At the very least, it's a courageous connection. In the meantime, Macey is reaching out to other organizations that connect to her passion for communication and helping others.

Remember Bonnie, the high school student who made the courageous connection with a university professor after reading his article in the *New York Times*? She was offered a position that didn't even exist. Professor Ovis created an opening just for her based on her unwavering passion.

Mary Reilly is a voice-over talent, copywriter, and morning radio co-host of the show "Liz & Reilly" on 94.5 Mix FM. She has worked in radio since 1987, in Tucson and Phoenix, Arizona, in towns all across the Midwest, and now in Eugene, Oregon. She's had the opportunity to interview rock stars, movie stars, and governors, but one of her favorite achievements has been proving that a two-woman morning show can be successful. Mary still loves her job every day, and even speaks this passion by saying as much in her LinkedIn bio.

Her long-term goal in radio was to run an alternative music show of her own. According to Mary, getting there wasn't a complex equation, "part of it was timing, but part of it was [to] *ask for it.*" By simply speaking her passion and making the ask, she got the show. In fact, the Grammy award-winning band, They Might Be Giants, was her very first interview.

"I'm a woman of great fortune because I've had amazing things happen. One thing I have continually done is pursue what I want," Mary said. "And I have found in life that I find what I'm looking for."

Since then, she's continued her passion career journey. When I asked her what's it's like working in her passion, she recalled a time when she started to take this for granted. "I was complaining to a friend... 'I have to get up from my nap and interview Stevie Nicks again...'" But Mary hearing herself say that out loud, she realized how grateful she is for her career and opportunities. "I don't *have* to... I *get* to go back to work and speak to a very gracious woman for the second year in a row."

Speaking your passion and making "the ask" today allows you to set the stage for when the timing is right. It's unlikely that the first day you decide to look for a job you'll find a posting for your dream gig. But why wait until all the stars align?

You get the gist: You can apply when there's nothing to apply for and you can ask for what you want. You're seeking future opportunities; you're putting yourself out there. You're doing something most people would never think to do.

Nathan Young, founder of Greater Good Storytelling, remembers not being too worried about his career while enrolled at the University of California, San Diego. He majored in history because of his passion for reading, writing, tackling big ideas, and understanding human nature. Since this was the 90s, though, Nathan figured he would jump into the dot-com boom and everything would work itself out.

After graduation, Nathan did end up working at a dot-com for a while. With the collapse of the bubble, though, he suddenly found himself out of work. He worked for two years as a firefighter for the U.S. Forest Service, but later realized he wanted to get back to his passions.

"It wasn't until my late 20s that I really started to question and think about what I wanted to do career-wise," he said.

Nathan had a portfolio of writing clips from a previous journalism internship and decided to make a bold move: pitch his writing to a Portland newspaper by pretending he had a meeting with the editor. He wasn't interested in waiting around for a job posting and wading through the traditional application process.

While he *was* able to hand over his portfolio, he didn't land the writing job.

The next day, Nathan received a call from the newspaper's sales team. They were impressed by his initiative and asked him to join the company in a sales role. In this position, Nathan learned the ins and outs of the advertising business, which, to his surprise, he loved.

Just like in Nathan's case, not every job opportunity is black and white. Some companies don't follow formal interview processes. Sometimes organizations don't have the capacity or time to orchestrate review committees.

This is especially true for smaller companies. Hiring processes at companies with fewer than 50 employees can range from formal to very informal. Either way, these companies are psyched on passionate people who reach out and demonstrate their interest. They beat the employer to the punch; they assess the need before the need is even communicated through a job post. It can be a challenge for some company directors to even find the time to create and market that post, regardless of how badly they need it.

What's more enticing, having someone reach out to you on an ordinary day because they've been interested in you for months, or someone replying to a specific opportunity that you posted and they randomly stumbled upon? I'd say the former is absolutely the type of bold person I'd want to work with as an employer.

Extreme makeover: cover letter edition

If you're wondering why I haven't mentioned the cover letter (the oft-dreaded job application element), it's because my hope is you will be so well-versed in speaking your passion that your letter will flow from your fingertips without any hesitation. If you are working on creating your personal brand and you've written down your story in the chapters above, your cover letter is basically copy and paste.

If you're still freaking out about the cover letter—I've been there—let me help ease your mind.

Your cover letter is simply a written version of speaking your passion. It has the added bonus of showing your potential employer that you have strong communication skills and can do more than just string a couple sentences together.

While your resume boasts your qualifications, your cover letter explains how you will use them to contribute to the organization.

Step 1: Format

Your cover letter is going to be three to four paragraphs, single-spaced with space in between paragraphs. Your cover letter should never exceed one page. Include your address and contact information at the top and begin with a formal greeting (Dear Mr./Ms.). Because you've already made the courageous connection with the employer, you should already know who you're addressing your cover letter to.

If for some reason that isn't possible, you should at the very least look online to find the name of the person who reviews applications. Search the organization's website for a human resources representative or someone in the same department as the listed position. If neither are available, you can use a standard greeting, "Dear Hiring Manager," "Dear Human Resources Director," or "To whom it may concern."

Step 2: Intro

There are two introduction options: traditional or creative.

For a traditional opening, state your interest in the position and introduce yourself with details such as your current position in your career or your education (university, year, and major). Be sure to include the position title you desire with something along the lines of, "I would like to express my interest in the Editor's position" or "I'm excited about the opportunity to apply for the Research Assistant position." You should show that you've researched the company and explain why you are passionate about the position (more on this in Step 3).

When it comes to your options for a creative introduction, Cady Heron said it best; the limit does not exist. Snag your employer's attention with a unique first line that speaks to the position or begin with an anecdote that relates to the field. This is your chance to stun an employer with your writing skills and ability to think outside the box. For example, a student applying for a public relations position may decide to tell the story of how he ran a relay race philanthropy event for his fraternity and after pitching the story to the school newspaper, which publicized the event and helped attract over 50 participants, he was hooked on the power of publicity.

Step 3: Research

Employers want to hear what draws you to their organization. This is your opportunity to brag about your passion. Your cover letter should sound as though you've been fantasizing about working at *that specific company* ever since you took a field trip to their factory in the 5th grade (obvi, only say that if it's true). Read the company's mission statement, client list, success stories, and press releases. Once you have a solid understanding of what the position with the company entails, you can further express your interest in working there. For example, "I'm passionate about your mission to keep our community informed about new developments in our education system and raise money for startup charter schools. By creating greater community involvement through the position of Events Coordinator, I am eager to help build more opportunities for children." Show off your research in the intro or middle paragraphs of your cover letter.

Step 4: Experience & contributions

What sets you apart from the competition? "Don't be afraid to discover what makes you different and then leverage what makes you different," said Jon Berghoff. "That's ultimately where you're probably going to find the intersection between what you're good at, what you enjoy, and what can make a difference in the world."

Connect the dots between your intentional experiences and the position you're applying to. Employers can look at your resume to see that you were the editor in chief of your college newspaper, so in the cover letter you'll need to explain just how that experience qualifies you to be an assistant editor for Flamingo Magazine. Explain that by leading 30 student journalists you learned the importance of building a team, delegating projects, and setting realistic deadlines.

Tell them what you bring to the table. You might want to describe your experience launching multi-media stories for the graduation issue of the school paper. Be as specific as possible—describe how the article was released on the homepage with images of funky graduation caps, which led readers to the website to watch the graduation video, which linked to the Twitter page for readers to tweet their graduation cap design ideas. While it's tempting to tell the employer what you will gain from the position—don't do it. For example, *do not* say something like, "I'm interested in this position so you can teach me how to become a stronger editor." While it's important to communicate your interest in learning and growth, the mindset of the employer isn't always one of teaching. Stay focused on what you can do for them, not what they can do for you.

Step 5: Thank you & interview

Employers may be sifting through dozens of cover letters, so always thank them for their time. Then, make it easy for them to contact you for an interview by signing off with some version of, "I have enclosed my resume for your review. Please feel free to contact me at 543-421-5435 and amanda@findyourpassioncareer.com. Thank you in advance for your time and consideration. I look forward to hearing from you soon." Then end with "Sincerely" and your name.

Example Format:

Street Address
City, State Zip

Date

Company Name
Company Street Address
Company City, State Zip

Dear Human Resources Director,

Paragraph 1: Introduction & Research

Paragraph 2: Research, Experience & Contributions

Paragraph 3: More Experience & Contributions

Paragraph 4: Thanks & Interview

Sincerely,
Your Name

Before you send in your cover letter, double check your spelling and grammar and get as much feedback as you can from your mentors first. Your cover letter can make or break your application, so make sure it's reviewed by those who know best—especially those in your desired field who have written successful cover letters and know what employers want to see.

In the traditional job-hunting mindset, many people think that sending in your resume and cover letter is the end game. But I can't tell you how many resumes and cover letters get sent out and fall into the black hole of an inbox. If you've applied to many jobs before, you know that this is true.

Some take this radio silence as them swiping left. Don't.

If you treat the cover letter as just another step in speaking your passion, you'll understand that there is much more communication that needs to happen for doors to open. Writing can convey the emotion that you feel when it comes to your passion. As someone who is passionate about writing, I believe that writing your passion can be very powerful.

But I also strongly believe that *speaking* your passion is another level of communication that ignites all the senses and is truly the key to getting the job you want. The way you appear and communicate your story and convey your passion at the interview is the real way in.

Up until this point you've crushed it at identifying your passion and writing the heck out of it. The interview is basically just doing this all out loud; you're storytelling and speaking your passion.

To improve your storytelling, lean on your parents, your mentors, and, the person who knows you best, your BFF. The best way to recognize your moments of greatness is to step outside of your own self and the way that you frame the stories of your life. Sometimes your highlight reel can fade because of your own impression of who you are. Think, WWMBFFS? (What Would My BFF Say?) In some cases, other people in your life can describe you better than you can describe yourself.

Imagine if Dan Kuhn, the editor in chief at *College Magazine* and recent graduate, had just straight up asked me for feedback on his storytelling skills before he interviewed? He might have saved himself several months of struggling through unsuccessful job interviews.

"Perception is everything. There's your own perception of yourself and then there's what other people see in you," said Kari Gold, senior HR operations partner at the Association of American Medical Colleges. "It's important to learn about how people see you, what your strengths are, and what your weaknesses are. Everyone has areas of development opportunities."

Claire Kreger-Boaz, a senior project manager for the National Association of Music Merchants (NAMM) Public Affairs and Government Relations and The NAMM Foundation, leaned on her friends and network for honest feedback when she felt lost in her career. "All of the points at which I was at a crossroads, I reached out to someone," said Claire.

She began her career journey at Montclair State University as an English literature major. She had a love for poetry, romanticism, and lyricism and wanted to create things that gave people a similar feeling to what she experienced when studying the subjects she treasured most. Although she was actively writing her own poetry and work, when she graduated, she couldn't see how this passion would translate into a career.

"I still didn't know how to channel this desire for artistic expression with [the] real world, needing to earn money," Claire said.

After going to bartending school and moving to Alaska—documenting her experience all the while—she made her way to San Diego where she worked as a production assistant for Greenhaven Press. In this position, she finally felt she was able to integrate creativity into her career.

She worked her way up in that company until she left to work for a well-known literary agent. However, she realized the intense, cutthroat environment was not the experience or career path she wanted for herself.

"I wasn't living my truth of how I wanted this world to be," she said.

Claire then returned to the Greenhaven Press family under Blackbirch Press as a content editor. She moved on to work in higher education as an associate sponsoring editor, where she managed over a million-dollar budget for producing learning products and e-textbooks. She admired her work. However, 2014 brought with it big cuts for the company, and Claire found herself included in the wave. This unexpected turn left Claire feeling lost in her career journey.

Shocked and with no idea of what her next career move would be, she approached friends, family, and even casual acquaintances to ask for feedback on how they viewed her strengths.

She told them, "I need a little help rebuilding my self-confidence. Tell me the qualities that you see in me that could possibly transfer to another type of career." The feedback she received helped her change her thought process in what skills she possessed and how they could transfer to other career paths.

"I learned how to talk about my skills instead of saying, 'I'm an editor'; 'I'm a writer'; or 'I'm a publisher,'" she said. "I started to be able to say, 'I'm a content creator'; 'I know how to curate content'; and 'I'm a project manager.'"

This new language and mindset led her to NAMM/The NAMM Foundation, where she was able to connect the dots of her content and management expertise in a project management role.

At The 2019 NAMM Show, Claire led the foundation in creating a one-of-a-kind experience in which students and music educators had the opportunity to sing along with iconic Grammy Award-winning composer Eric Whitacre. Claire explains she considers her work something she "gets to do" rather than "has to do." If that's not the definition of *living the dream* I'm not sure what is.

I was fortunate enough to attend The NAMM Show and I felt chills in that moment, singing with the entire room of people passionate about music with Eric Whitacre and his Virtual Choir.

"What I get to do is give people an experience like that," Claire said. "They walk out of the room and say, 'That was a spiritual experience for me.'"

At any point in your career journey, especially at the start, meet with your college advisor. Talk to your family, friends, mentors, and especially your best friends, about how they would describe you and your strengths. It may sound silly, but it's important to interview your inner circle of family and friends to fully understand how your strengths are perceived.

If you already feel confident about your strengths, then ask for feedback on your storytelling. Think of Dan. He knew that he had a lot of experience as the editor in chief at *College Magazine*, but the way he told the story didn't highlight his strengths. It wasn't until he asked me how I would describe his role that he could see how impactful he was.

We're all guilty of underselling ourselves. We're not as kind to ourselves as we are to our friends, but why?

ACTION:

Picture your BFF and write down how you would describe them.

Most likely you gave your friend a very praise-filled description. We're more likely to praise and lift up our friends than we are to view ourselves with that glass-half-full mentality. It's easier to see all the greatness in those we love most.

I took my own challenge and asked my BFF about my strengths. I met Kari Gold, my best friend, 15 years ago as a counselor at Blue Star Summer Camps. According to Kari, my top three strengths are that I am driven, I would do anything for my friends, and I have the ability to make every day fun.

It feels absolutely incredible to hear such kind feedback from someone I admire and care about. I'm not certain I would have considered any of these strengths myself and hearing them from a pal and a confidant makes me realize that this is how I'm perceived. It also makes me understand what parts of my personality are impressive to others. Something such as drive can be described through a story during an interview, and that story could prove that I'd go to infinity and beyond to get the job done.

For most of us, it can be a challenge to brag about ourselves like we can about our friends. I've seen this in even the brightest students, including the very impressive Bonnie from Reality Changers.

Bonnie was writing a college application essays on her ability to be resourceful. As I read her essay, prepared to give feedback, I realized I was left with quite a few questions. Why did she have to become resourceful or showcase her resourcefulness? What was the context for this trait?

Bonnie comes from a low-income background and when she was going into high school, she wanted a more challenging academic environment than what her current school offered. She applied and was selected as one of only five candidates from her middle school to attend a high-performing school outside of her district.

Upon attending her new high school, she learned that she lacked the resources her peers had access to, like tutors and expensive after-school programs to supplement their education. Nevertheless, she persisted and found free opportunities to get help with her studies, like meeting with her teachers after class. Today she's in the top 15 percent of her class.

Being resourceful is 100 percent a significant skill. But the real accomplishment was Bonnie's ability to go from a struggling student in a new environment to slaying her studies in the top 15 percent of her class. She was actively clawing her way to the top after starting from the bottom.

Like Bonnie, so many of us overlook how impressive we are. We distill our finest qualities to the most general terms. Why?

The answer is simple: We hang out with ourselves all day long. We find our strengths mundane since we're using them day in and day out. But real talk, everyone has impressive stories to tell. Take a minute to recognize your worth and tell your story the right way.

Once you realize how to tell your story properly, practice it on repeat in the form of a mock interview. Hand your BFF a series of questions to ask you, and practice answering them. If this practice round sounds cringe worthy, imagine how you'll feel answering these questions come interview day.

I've sat down with friends and students who initially felt they nailed their interviews, but once I ask follow-up questions, they reveal even stronger answers. Employers won't necessarily be asking these follow-ups during the interview, so you need to make sure you've achieved storytelling clarity within your answer on the first take.

Make sure that you convey a feeling, something beyond your words—your passion, your emotion, your desire for this role and organization. Ask your friend: Can you feel how passionate I am about this opportunity? Make sure the answer is a resounding *yes*.

Interview like a boss

An interview request means that the employer believes that you're qualified. Don't get it twisted though, this does not mean you're the best person for the role.

The interview is the most important time to speak your passion. Future employers are not mind readers. Even if they've seen your incredible portfolio or are in awe at your resume, they need to hear the passion directly from you. But don't worry; you've been practicing and you are ready.

Of course, this is a lot easier said than done, especially if you're shy or introverted. But you'll find that if you start speaking your passion in random conversations and mock interviews with friends and family, people you're comfortable with, the easier it gets.

When you interview, take your time. Be sure to get as specific as possible. In other words, when you speak your passion, don't assume the listener fully understands your story, your history, your actions, or your timeline.

Here's the tea, the piping hot matcha that no one else will admit at the fear of sounding stupid: Most job positions are kind of confusing.

Do you ever feel lost when someone tells you about a company they work for and some general title they hold? We're oftentimes confused about what they actually do or what their company represents, but we're too afraid to question them. Like, what even is the assistant to the regional manager?

Since I love understanding other people's careers and I think it's important to get curious, I ask follow-up questions like, "What's a day in your work life like?" or "What's your favorite part of the job?"

Don't assume just anyone will do what I do, though; in fact, they probably won't. You need to break down exactly what your experience is for interviewers—even if they don't explicitly ask.

If they're confused about what exactly you did in the day-to-day as the PR person for your service fraternity, they may not ask and they may make the wrong assumptions. They may not know that service fraternities aren't the same thing as social fraternities. They may not understand that by being involved with this service fraternity, you've demonstrated your passionate for the environment. They won't know that you spent an entire semester on a project helping your local community through initiatives like the community garden you helped build. Perhaps you even chose the variety of vegetables and you remember how it felt to see your hard work result in carrots, beets, and kale to give back to local families in need.

You truly have to radiate your passion when you speak if you want to start connecting the dots between you and a career. The more confident you feel when it comes to your passion and abilities, the better you are able to speak about your passion during an interview.

As much as I wish I could, I can't just fork over this confidence to you. But what I can do is remind you how crucial it is to start treating yourself better so that you can finally grasp how truly qualified you are.

Patricia Moreno is the founder of Spiritual Fitness, leading a conversation about exercising our own power and the importance of positive self-talk and raising consciousness.

Patricia had struggled with her own body image, having been placed on a diet since she was eight years old. By the time she was 12, Patricia weighed more than 200 lbs. But from the moment she took her first dance aerobics class in high school, she knew this was her passion.

Fitness gave her back her control over her outward appearance, but her mindset was still fixated on her body image. "[I thought my image] would determine how people felt about me or the level of success I would have," she said. That mentality took her down a dark path.

After improving her level of fitness, Patricia achieved her "dream body image" and started on an incredibly successful career path, receiving sponsorships from Nike and Reebok. But she felt like a sellout because she wasn't actually living healthy; she was starving herself, binging and purging and relying on drugs. "My mantra was thin at any cost," she said.

After a breakdown, she finally realized that the vicious cycle of diet and exercise in which she was entwined wasn't the answer. "It wasn't me that was wrong. It was the recipe that was wrong," said Patricia.

Her challenge wasn't physical; it was spiritual. "You can't change how you feel about yourself by changing your circumstances," she said. "That's an inside job."

That's why she developed a workout program that shifts how we see ourselves and helps participants master their emotions. It took years of training and studying with personal optimization experts, mindset scholars, and spiritual teachers until Patricia Moreno eventually created her own practices called intenSati and The Evolution, which are designed to integrate spiritual fitness into the lives of hundreds of thousands worldwide.

Patricia's practice helps others break through negative thinking and become intentional thinkers. When you love yourself, you begin to believe in yourself and remind yourself of how powerful and great you are—just the way your BFF would talk about you.

"Then you would go to those interviews and be like 'this is what I bring, this is what I'm willing to learn, this is how I'm willing to grow'—and that excitement and that passion is what people want to buy into," said Patricia.

You can even speak your passion to carve your own path, outside of the formal interview process.

For example, when the road in front of Barbara Bry's office fell into disrepair, she felt strongly about finding a better system to fix it. She spoke about this so frequently her daughter suggested she run for city council.

Lisa Rosenfelt spoke of her passion for community, and by speaking her passion, she created Ivy Street, a co-working space.

Natalie Janji spoke her passion for morning routines to Hal Elrod, the author of *The Miracle Morning*, and ultimately convinced him that she was the best person for the opportunity to write *The Miracle Morning for College Students*.

It's no easy feat to win that position on city council, launch your own business, or connect with a famous author. It takes determination, passion, and intentional steps.

Not to mention, when you get that first rejection—and you *will* face rejection—you may start to question everything. Even just one little "no" can feel like an avalanche on your career journey climb. But you must be resilient.

Continuing to speak your passion, regardless of how many times you hear "no" or even hear nothing at all, can help you achieve resiliency. When you understand your own story and you share it, you ultimately grow and become stronger. "By sharing your stories, you become more courageous, become more resilient, become more compassionate," said Nathan Young, founder of Greater Good Storytelling.

Nathan turned his fondness of storytelling into his current business. "Getting used to really sharing who I was and putting myself out there in a way that was vulnerable—primarily through storytelling—connected me with so many people and connected me with myself in a way that wasn't happening before," he said.

By speaking his passion, people started asking him to teach the art of storytelling at their organizations. Today he gets to encourage individuals and organizations to better share their mission through storytelling.

"If you get to a point in your life where you feel comfortable sharing very vulnerable stories about yourself, there is a lot of power and a lot of strength that comes from that," he said.

Now what exactly will they ask you at the interview? I'm not a psychic, but I can share with you some of the most popular questions asked during job interviews based on research and experience. Let's look to one of our beautifully researched articles on *College Magazine*, written by Amelia Lytle and Patience Kayira:

1. **What skills do you have that make you qualified for this job position?**

   You'll definitely want to bring specific examples to the table. AbbVie Inc. employee Lisa Filar is the director of compliance and holds extensive interviews for her team. "I'm looking for candidates who can articulate their contributions to a solution. Typically, superstar candidates can be very specific about what they personally did as part of a team," said Filar.

2. **When was a time that you showed leadership skills?**

   Everyone looks for leadership qualities in a hire. It can mean anything from being president of a club to organizing a group project for a class. Kelly Barnett, director of career development at the S.I. Newhouse School of Public Communications at Syracuse University, explains that the best option is to use examples that relate to the position you want so the interviewer can see how your past experience will help with your future. "Draw parallels between yourself and the job description. This shows preparedness, as you clearly know what the job is looking for and how to show this in your past experiences," said Barnett.

3. **Tell me about a time you failed to meet an objective.**

Being able to talk about how you failed in the past, and how you came out stronger and better prepared afterwards says a lot about how you work. Interviewers use this question to catch people off guard. People who prepped to show their strong points may not have thought about their weak points as much. "Lots of people hate talking about failures, but showing your interviewers you have self-awareness is vital," said Barnett.

Talking about weaknesses also shows how you've learned from these experiences. "There is no perfect candidate, so if someone says that they don't have any weaknesses, that is a red flag for me. We all can improve on some aspect of ourselves," said Filar. Follow this up with how your failure helped you grow and what you did to prevent it from happening again. The only thing better than self-awareness is self-improvement.

4. **What prior experience do you have with____?**

If you just hit the job market, this can feel like a killer. You may feel like you have nothing to say because you haven't held a professional job before, or even a job in a similar field, but keep in mind that any work experience or experience with leadership in a club or activity will teach you helpful skills you need for the job. "When I was interviewed for a job at the clothing store Lester's, they asked about my previous experience and, not having any previous sales associate jobs, I instead talked about my experience babysitting. I related working with kids to being able to successfully engage the clothing store's target audience," said Syracuse University student Sydney Kaplan. Draw connections between experiences to show your preparation for the new role.

5. Tell me about yourself.

Does the employer want your autobiography—the embarrassing elementary school accidents, hopeless high school crushes, medical history, and more? No. "Be concise—30 seconds to one minute," said assistant director at Smith College's Lazarus Center for Career Development Janice Schell. The employer just wants a brief insight on you as a person.

This question demonstrates the employer's interest in getting to know you. Kind of like when your friend's cat rubs its furry head against your leg— a gesture of friendship. "Reframe this question in the context of being in [the specific] role at our organization," said Schell. Breaking it up will help you hone your answer and prevent you from rambling.

At the same time, being put on the spot to talk about yourself can be challenging. "I find this a very tricky question mostly because I am awkward and I hate talking about myself," says Smith College alum Hilda Nalwanga. The fear of sounding "prideful" makes many people afraid to answer this question. To avoid feeling lost at sea with this question, Schell offers this basic framework:

▷ Who you are right now (class year, school, degree, major, minor)

▷ A recent experience (specific project, job, internship, extracurricular) of relevance/benefit to the employer
▷ A previous supporting experience
▷ Why this opportunity? What are you searching for in a position? Any question/s for the employer?

Thinking about yourself in terms of class year and previous work experiences will help you tackle this question with concision and grace. Who knows? It may make it easier for you to answer the bigger question—who are you?

6. Why should I hire you?

Channel the confidence you had when you walked up to Chad at the last fraternity party and make yourself sound as interesting and qualified as possible. This question makes it easier for an employer to make their hiring decision. "It's a quick way to gauge whether or not the interviewee is the right fit for a company," said Smith College student and Lazarus Center peer advisor Michelle Chen. Employers see a ton of applicants, and they want to pick people who will vibe well with the organization.

In the face of a question like this, be confident and sell yourself. Humbleness shouldn't prevent you from talking about your strengths. Ask yourself, "What makes you different from the other applicants?" Maybe you have a unique perspective, ability to take risks, or a range of experiences that not many other candidates would have on their resumes. "The best approach is to avoid the trite answers of 'I work hard' and 'I'm determined and I will never give up,'" said Chen. Cheesy answers may get you far on Tinder, but they won't help you in an interview. Everyone has something that sets them apart—you just have to find yours and use it to your advantage.

7. Why shouldn't I hire you?

Think carefully about this answer, or you may get kicked off the island. This question feels like a trap because it is a trap. In order to get out of the rabbit hole, you have to get into the rabbit hole. "Stay calm. If an applicant is unsure of how to answer immediately, the worst thing to do would be to charge ahead blindly or say, 'I don't know,'" said associate director for Internship Programs at Amherst College Victoria Wilson. Taking time to think about your answer does not show weakness; it shows thoughtfulness.

When an employer asks a question like this, they may want to know if you can remain composed and confident. They also might use this question to see how you describe your strengths and weaknesses. "If a position states a preference for a major which isn't offered at your school, explain why your major and other background are assets, and express genuine enthusiasm to learn content you may not know," said Schell. Acknowledging what you don't know can lead you somewhere. Being able to pinpoint the reasons why you shouldn't be hired also shows self-awareness.

8. Tell me something about yourself that is not on your resume.

Spontaneity. Don't get taken aback by this one. Interviews are conversations. An interviewer may ask this question to learn about your other interests. Show the employer that your passions extend beyond the world of work. The Lazarus Center encourages students and recent grads to keep their resumes up to a page. If you're going into teaching or writing a CV, then it's acceptable to have a two-page resume.

A resume only gives a snapshot of your professional history. The information we omit still says a lot about ourselves. If you think your vintage tea-cup obsession that got you made fun of in middle school won't ever help you, think again. Your interviewer may also share an affinity for Victorian china, ultimately helping you to land the job.

9. **Describe a specific instance where you conformed to a policy with which you did not agree.**

Forcing yourself to attend that grueling 9:00 a.m. because of the professor's mandatory attendance policy doesn't count as a good answer to this common question. It may be better to talk about that time you stayed an extra two hours for your newspaper's layout and editing night. Even though you were exhausted and stressed about your classes the next day, you stayed to help your team. An answer like this shows off your ability to prioritize the needs of your team.

Questions like this are intended to assess how you act in certain situations. To tackle it, try the STAR method. S for stating the situation, T for identifying the task, A for explaining the action you took, R for describing the results of you achieved. "The STAR approach structures interview answers well and prevents me from rambling," Chen says. This method also helps you reflect over your experiences. During your interview prep, try breaking down your experiences with the STAR model and see what you can come up with.

10. **What were some of your greatest obstacles in getting here today?**

Challenges and failure speak a lot about your work-ethic. Do you get discouraged? Or do you persist? As Nalwanga says,

"With questions about failure, I try to balance honesty about my failures and mistakes with how badass I am—I talk about how I failed and then how I overcame that failure, as well as what I took away from it and did differently when a similar situation happened." Like many of the questions on this list, keep your response positive.

11. What are your salary expectations?

This question is daunting. But doing research on the company and the role will give you a good idea of what figure to say. The Lazarus Center advises students to take caution when asked about salaries and benefits during an interview. The center also recommends that if the employer brings up salary, give the range you've researched. A range, rather than a specific number, makes you appear willing to negotiate.

Here's an example of a response: "I understand that the expected range for this role falls between X to Y, and because of my experience and skills I'd like to be at the higher end of the range."

12. Give me an example of a time you were able to communicate successfully with another person even when that individual might not have liked you or vice versa.

At some point, we've all had to work with people we didn't like. But you got the project done, broke through differences with communication, right? Focus on how you made that happen. A question like this requires you to think about your communication and collaboration skills. Again, employers want to hire someone who will contribute to a peaceful, productive work environment.

Questions about the company:

13. What are your ideas on how we can improve ____?

As a potential employee, the company wants to see what you in particular can bring to the table. Start by thinking about new ideas for a product or service, or even how you'll bring a fresh perspective to the company. "The uniqueness in your ideas will make you stand out from the rest of the applicants and bring you to the top of their list," said Barnett.

14. What are you looking for in your next job?

You want this specific job for a reason. You didn't just randomly point at a list and apply to something on a whim. Talk about why you want this position in particular. Filar explained this is one of her favorite questions to ask to see if applicants are passionate and if the job will fit what they are looking for. "Someone should be able to articulate the top five things they want out of their next job," said Filar. For this question, make sure the job description meets your goals, and also how it'll help you, personally. Here's the time to show your passion—make sure they know why you really want this job.

Practice these questions and you'll slay any interview: you'll share your passion, establish that you are an exceptional potential hire, and demonstrate that you go above and beyond by asking thoughtful questions that you've written down in advance. Don't rely on your awesome improv skills here if you don't have to; I know you may think you can just wing it, but it's more notable to show up prepared.

ACTION:

Write down your answers to these questions so you can start practicing. Then prepare questions for the person who will be interviewing you.

If this sounds familiar to the questions you've prepared during your courageous connections, that's because they should—you nailed it. Just like when you're researching a potential mentor, you've researched this company and you've prepared questions to demonstrate your interest and prove that you've done your homework about the organization's mission.

Don't forget, working for your dream company is a two-way street. Asking questions about the company and job will earn you brownie points with a potential employer but will also give you the information you need to ensure that this is in fact the job you thought it was. Here are a couple example questions you can ask:

1. What do you love most about working here?
2. What are your goals for this position (or long-term vision for the organization), and how will you measure success?
3. What are some of the greatest challenges I may experience in the position?
4. What characteristics are most important for success in this role?
5. Can you describe some ways in which there are opportunities for this position to help improve the organization?

Apply from the Upside Down

Just as I've asked you to rethink your career journey, I'm now going to ask you to switch up the way you apply for jobs. Your mantra should no longer be: "One job application a day keeps unemployment away." Now, you should be repeating to yourself: "Researching one company and making one courageous connection a day gets you on your way to your dream career." (Okay, okay, that may be a bit long-winded for a mantra, but you get the point.)

Lily Maslia, a journalism student at The Ohio State University, shared that she's stressing about not finding any job she loves. She's afraid she'll end up bored no matter where she's working. "Should I just stop blindly applying places online and instead work to make physical and interpersonal connections in order to find a job?" she asked me. The answer is a resounding yes, 100 percent! Especially if you want a job you love.

If you need just any job, get a job. Even if you ultimately want a career you love but need a job in the meantime, find work. Everyone has bills to pay. There's no shame in the game.

But if you're ready to start your intentional career journey, follow this process, speak your passion like your life depends on it, and doors will open. It's a different mentality; instead of a feeling of scarcity (telling yourself the only jobs out there are the ones on Indeed.com right now) versus one of opportunity and attraction (my dream career exists, and I'm on a journey to discover, connect, and achieve it). You can, you will, you must.

I say "upside-down job application" because it's the reverse of what people think they should be doing. Instead of seeking the job post, applying, and getting the job and *then* getting to know the company, you're going to learn about the company and potential future co-workers and assignments first before even learning what role you might play in the organization.

If you have all the free time in the world, you could bulk-up your research and courageous connections right this second. But to do this while still working your current job or finishing school, you must treat your career journey like a final research project. Minus the existential crisis at 11:59pm. Every day we're going to put in work and get closer to accomplishing the final product, the project, the paper; or, in this case, the job offer.

If you are in for the slow and steady approach, here's how you can make steady progress on your intentional career journey:

Step 1: Research

Every day look up one company or organization that you think sounds incredible.

Step 2: Connect

Track down an employee who works there and connect courageously— send that LinkedIn message and email.

Step 3: Repeat

Repeat, repeat, repeat. Every damn day.

Alexandra Blackwell, my graduating editor in chief at *College Magazine*, spoke to me recently about her career vision. She followed this very process. She's passionate about theater and communications, so she reached out to the general manager of Theatre Jax and then to the managing director at The 5 and Dime. She then diligently added them to her little black Excel workbook of courageous connections. Yes, you heard right; she's maintaining an actual Excel spreadsheet to make this a serious assignment—because it's an intentional career journey and it requires the level of diligence you would give to a research project.

Once you've sent that connection message like Alexandra, follow up. If you don't hear back again, follow up. It never hurts to message more than once or twice. Don't be a stage five clinger, but let it be known that you're an eager beaver. Then once you've held an informational interview, follow up again to say thank you (as you should with anyone who helps you on your career journey).

I can't stress this enough: It is *so* important to stay in touch. Make yourself center stage of their mind at all times.

Through her courageous connections, Alexandra was offered a communications internship at Players by the Sea Theatre. Then after a couple months she applied and was accepted for a full position as the marketing and communications manager.

"It really is a dream come true! It feels so good to be starting my career journey in the theatre world while putting my communication and writing skills to good use," said Alexandra.

Most importantly, if someone gives you their time, whether it's through helpful feedback on your resume or cover letter, connecting for an informational interview, or a job interview, always send a thank you email. I can't tell you how much this will separate you from everyone else who felt like a thank you email was a frivolous idea or who never even considered sending one in the first place.

Not certain where to start with your thank you note? Follow TABSE, an acronym which Rima Kikani breaks down in her article on *College Magazine*:

> **Thank you:** Thank the interviewer for meeting with you and relay your enthusiasm about the possibility of working for the

organization you applied to. If this is a competitive position with numerous applicants, mention the date of your interview and the position for which you applied.

Admire: Maybe you met some very intelligent people. Maybe you were impressed by the workplace structure. Or maybe you felt energized by the challenging opportunity of the role. Praise the company and make it believable.

Brag: Review your qualifications and what makes you the perfect candidate for the position. Briefly discuss why you would be successful. Professional writer Alice Feathers said, "You might want to mention an interesting topic or rewarding moment from your interview."

Second chance: If you forgot to mention something during the interview or just thought of something else, here's your chance. "[This is] an opportunity to answer or further address any question you felt you didn't cover well in the interview; the brilliance that occurred to you in the elevator ride down to your car after you left the office," said author Christine Hassler. Don't miss it again.

Echo: Thank your interviewer one more time for considering you for the position. Reiterate yourself as a valuable candidate and finally, let him or her know that you look forward to hearing back soon.

Keep your note short and sweet…and sincere. No one wants to read three pages frosted with lies, and they will be able to tell. Remember to send your thank you note within 24 hours of your interview.

10

STARTED FROM THE
BOTTOM NOW WE'RE HERE

D id you know that millennials rate leadership as the most prized
skill to develop in order to achieve career success? I couldn't agree
more! Full disclosure, I'm a millennial too. Or an "elder millennial,"
according to the hilarious comedian Iliza Shlesinger in her Netflix
special.

While leadership is most prized, only 24% of millennials believe
that this is a strong personal trait of theirs upon graduation, and 63%
have said their leadership skills aren't fully developed by their company.
These stats are all according to Deloitte's survey in 2017.[25]

With that said, leadership is a key element of your career journey
at *any* stage, whether you're in your first job, fifth, or even if you've
never held a job.

This final chapter on your intentional career journey is for everyone.
Introverts: leadership is for you too!

Yes, you heard me correctly, do I need to say it louder? Leadership isn't reserved for just the extroverted visionaries. Melissa Eisler,

a leadership and executive coach, feels that anyone can be a leader as long as they are willing to put in the work.

"Leadership is about motivating and influencing others toward a common purpose or goal. Strong leaders bring out the best in others and inspire them to grow, while working towards a common mission," she said. Leaders must build relationships and communicate effectively in order for that growth and vision to advance.

For example, if you're an editor at *College Magazine* leading a team of 10 writers, you may learn that one of your writers, Sarah, is struggling to find expert sources to interview for her articles. You may meet with Sarah to learn what's working for her and where she needs your help. You may walk her through your own process or others that you've had success with in the past. Then you can help Sarah set clear milestones for sealing the deal. You may also see that as a teaching moment to elevate the source-work of your entire team and help them all find higher-quality sources to improve their content. Meanwhile, through all of this you are bringing your best self by offering your guidance and expertise.

Some leadership roles require a visionary. Other leadership positions may require more of a manager, like leading a team to execute upon a determined vision. Similarly, some leadership roles may benefit from outgoing, social types whereas some leadership positions may not.

In other words, being a leader doesn't mean you're the loudest in the room. Being a leader can take a variety of forms.

If you're setting the vision for a company but you're more introverted, you may lead in a way that doesn't overwhelm you—like carefully making sure your calendar isn't crammed with too many meetings so you can still focus on the bigger picture. If you're managing a team of other introverted personalities, you may be even better off because you'll fully understand where they're coming from.

And you can start working on your leadership skills today. Yes, today.

"Don't wait for leadership opportunities to come your way; go and seek them out," Melissa said. "The more you practice being a leader, the better you'll be at it, just like anything in life."

Melissa is an International Coach Federation (ICF)-certified leadership and executive coach who partners with leaders, executives, and entrepreneurs to help them develop communication skills, prove organizational effectiveness, and become stronger, more present leaders. She blends 15 years of experience in the corporate world with her background in mindfulness to help her clients achieve new heights.

In fact, Melissa has created an intentional career journey for herself centered on her passions. After graduating from Lehigh University with a degree in journalism, Melissa started her career as a writer and editor for online publishers and landed in a role leading a content team in the health and wellness space. While there, she began teaching yoga and meditation within the company. As a side hustle, she led workshops around mindfulness for leaders and stress management in the corporate setting.

Following her passion for mindfulness, Melissa went on to work at the Chopra Center where she created content, developed editorial strategy, and managed a team. She decided to return to school to get certified as a coach and also get her graduate degree in organizational leadership. She now has a private leadership and executive coaching practice.

Melissa is devoted to helping others become more effective and inspiring leaders. She likens the role of a leader to that of an orchestra conductor—whose role is to create something bigger and better than the sum of its parts by bringing together the strengths of each musician and creating a shared vision.

So what exactly does it mean to be a leader?

"Being a leader means bringing everyone to work toward a common cause or common goal and to have that group functioning in a way that is creating something more meaningful than those individuals could ever create on their own," said Melissa. "That's so powerful."

Melissa advises leaders to not only be open to feedback but to seek it out: Surround yourself with people who will tell you the truth and be self-reflective to better understand your weaknesses and strengths. Even if this exercise is a not-so-hot reality check for you, embrace it. Just like you asked for feedback on your strengths in determining your career path, you want to ask for feedback on your leadership style.

"I think the strongest leaders recognize what they don't know and what they aren't good at and are able to ask for help when they need to," she said.

Connect with your mentors, friends, co-workers, and employers to better understand how you lead effectively and how you can improve.

Don't stop believing

A leadership position says, "I'm serious about this organization." You're not just an attendee, volunteer, or someone who shows up at the last minute to do whatever the boss asks of you.

A leadership position shows you genuinely care, you go the extra mile with your time and energy, you communicate effectively, and, most importantly, you inspire others.

Is there one organization you are a part of that aligns most with your passions? *That's* the one to grow within and take on a leadership role. Don't just take on more responsibility everywhere you look, especially if your heart's not in it.

Every now and then we'll have students who are completely qualified to take on editor duties at *College Magazine*, only to realize that they've spread themselves too thin and need to drop in favor of other commitments. It's not a fun moment for the student or the organization.

When you commit, commit fully—be certain that the organization is one you want to commit to.

In high school at the Carver Center for Arts and Technology, I took on the leadership role of vice president for the Key Club, a philanthropy organization. In this role, I helped organize the annual fundraiser. That year we decided to host a variety show. Saying I was stoked would be an understatement. The idea of creating a show from scratch, auditioning students to perform, and raising money through ticket sales had "Amanda Nachman" written all over it. And I knew that our artistic community at school would be the perfect fit for such a fundraiser.

Everyone in the Key Club helped by spreading word about the auditions, designing flyers, selling tickets, and organizing the microphones and speakers for the day of the performance. It was an amazing show; we even had a professor get involved to perform a rap. As the vice president, I helped orchestrate the event from concept to execution, and I got to emcee (score!).

You can't gain experience if you don't take on responsibilities. You have to jump in, raise your hand, and say, "I'm on top of it!" Then commit. Stick to your word.

If you're not a leader in the sense that you don't want to organize an event or delegate work to your team, consider positions that allow you to be a leader in a less spotlighted role. For example, maybe you want to lead in the design of the visual assets for your organization or manage the organization's budget in the treasurer position.

ACTION:

What organization can you take on a leadership position or grow as a leader in? Or what are some ways you can build your leadership skills? Write it down.

Find your Elaine Welteroth

One easy way to identify your own leadership style is to look to the leaders you admire most. How can you be more like them?

As the managing director of the Dingman Center for Entrepreneurship at the University of Maryland, Asher Epstein, my mentor, grew the program to exponential heights that could only be reached by a visionary with strong leadership skills.

Asher helped University of Maryland students—business majors, engineers, MBAs, and any entrepreneurial student who reached out to the Dingman Center—understand the very core of what it meant to be an entrepreneur: Find the problem.

He launched the Annual Cupid's Cup Competition by working with Kevin Plank, founder and CEO of Under Armour and University of Maryland alumnus. Kevin himself got his first taste of entrepreneurship as a student by selling roses across campus on Valentine's Day (hence the inspiration for "Cupid's Cup").

Asher and his team at The Dingman Center also engaged alumni to coach student entrepreneurs. Through his leadership and passion for entrepreneurship, Asher generated a lively community of students driven to launch businesses. This is a community I call home, even to this day. I still keep in touch with connections I made through the center, even more than 10 years out of college.

Another leader whose style has inspired me is California's Senate President pro Tempore Toni G. Atkins. When I launched the 50by2050 Project in 2017 with a goal of achieving 50 percent of women in congress by the year 2050, I reached out to Senator Atkins to meet with her and get her insights on the project.

When the day finally came to meet with Senator Atkins and her team, I was nervous; I had never worked with political leaders or met with a senator before. When I joined them at a conference table in her San Diego office, Senator Atkins immediately made me feel at home. In her words and demeanor, she is genuine and down to earth. She doesn't shy away from sharing her story and will tell you about her childhood growing up in a home without running water in Virginia. Her authenticity makes her relatable and that's one of the traits that I admire in a leader. I'm eternally grateful for her advice, which became a key element of the 50by2050 Project's vision. Senator Atkins said the missing puzzle piece to achieving parity in Congress is mentorship for young women leaders. Because of this, we're working now toward creating a mentorship program between congresswomen and a cohort of ambitious college women leaders.

Dr. Ken Blanchard is another leader worthy of mentioning. He's the author of *The One Minute Manager* and cofounder of The Ken Blanchard Companies, an international management training and consulting firm. In addition to being a renowned speaker, author, and consultant, Ken is a trustee emeritus of the Board of Trustees at his alma mater, Cornell University, and teaches students in the Master of Science in Executive Leadership Program at the University of San Diego.

I heard Blanchard speak in 2014. At the time, I was working at an advertising agency and was part of the creative team on a brand development project for The Ken Blanchard Companies. I went with the intention of learning more about my client, but I took home some invaluable leadership tools.

What stuck with me most about his talk was a piece of advice he gave for leaders who are experiencing problems with members of their team. He suggests that leaders should always try to remember the reasons they hired someone. If something's not working, spend time figuring out the cause of the issue versus jumping to a harsher conclusion—asking someone to resign or firing them. It's easy to want to give up on someone who isn't giving it their all. Remember the time you spent sharing your vision with that person and training that person. Remember the hopes and dreams you had for them. And lastly, remember that you grow by investing in your people.

By looking to leaders I admire, I've identified the kind of leader *I* want to be. I've measured my success by being the kind of leader—and human, for that matter—that makes me proud. That might sound a bit silly, but I only lead in a way that's authentic to who I am. I would never want to be the type of boss that I wouldn't want as my own supervisor. I don't want my people to feel like they can't approach me with anything. Like the great Michael Scott, I'd only want my team to be afraid of how much they love me. I strive to be a visionary like Asher, relatable like Toni, and committed to my team like Ken.

I want to be the leader that I find admirable; one who spreads positive energy throughout the team, sets exponential goals, and who not only asks for feedback, but who is ready to listen with an open mind.

One tangible way I demonstrate the kind of leader I want to be is by only giving assignments that I would take on myself. I want to show that I have my skin in the game. In other words, before I hired fraternity guys to hand-distribute my magazine, I hand-distributed thousands myself. By doing the job firsthand, I was able to understand exactly what was involved and appreciate the hard work before eventually hiring a professional distribution company.

By the time I assigned my editorial director to lead recruiting efforts and student interviews, I had already paved the way by interviewing hundreds of students myself and developing a strong recruiting system. I also keep an open mind for improvements to my systems; I trust my editorial director to build upon, or even redesign, the original and embrace her ownership over the process.

No matter how much our team grows, my skin stays in the game. If I'm going to ask a student to create a video, I'll show them that I'm not afraid to do it too. I'll even make the first one. This doesn't mean that I take the first stab at every imaginable task, but at the very least, I need to be willing to do anything I assign to others. I don't believe in delegating out any lowly, crummy task just for the sake of giving someone something to do. Every project must come back to our vision, our "why." We want to help college students be successful. It's the core of why I founded and continue to love *College Magazine*.

That's the next key of being a strong leader: Sharing the "why." Sharing the vision. Explaining how everyone's hard work is going to contribute to the big picture and make a significant impact on the organization.

If I have a tedious assignment that needs to be done, like building an email list, sending out dozens of individualized emails for press, or crafting recruiting messages, I always go back to the "why." Once everyone is connected through our vision, we can embrace and see the upside of just about anything—no matter how dull it may seem. But if a task doesn't connect to that vision, then it's a waste of time and it won't get assigned.

For example, if I'm going to ask our editorial director to conduct keyword research on financial literacy, it's because we have a larger vision for *College Magazine* to become an incredible guide to help students make smart financial decisions. From the keyword research, we'll gain an understanding of how students search for topics such as paying off student loans or getting their first credit card—even how credit works. Wouldn't you like to know?

From the keyword research we'll develop competitive article concepts and then allow our writers to choose the topics that pique their interests most. The research, competitive analysis, and formulation of article concepts is a challenging task—but when I assign it, it all threads back to the larger vision. And the goal is set: Can we develop a full vertical/section that answers students' financial questions by the end of the year? The larger vision is what makes it exciting, especially when the full project comes together.

A project like the one described sets our company up for success in partnering with finance-related services that college students should know about and the best savings accounts to start them on an intentional financial journey.

I also aim to be a leader who is grateful for everyone's hard work. I've had the exact opposite experience in the past with a former boss; imagine putting together a 20-page proposal only to get a half-enthusiastic "great job," followed by "but you misspelled a word on page 16." *Seriously?*

As an editor myself, I promise you it's easy to find that one mistake. It's easy to focus on what's wrong or what's missing. It's much harder to start off positive and give meaningful feedback that goes beyond an offhand "great job" that will land without any authentic specificity. Empty pats on the back will only encourage your team to start looking for new opportunities to flex their skills and talents.

This is especially true when it comes to working with any creator—someone who spends hours of their time creating an original piece of work, from writing an article or video script to designing a logo—it's important to show gratitude for their time and effort by giving *your* time to review that work properly. I only give feedback that shows I spent the time and effort to see the good in someone's hard work. And if someone didn't spend the time to deliver quality work, I'll make that case by simply asking: "How much time did you spend on this?" or "Can you give it more effort before I review?"

From there as a leader you want to encourage what's working; what that person is doing well. If you can foster talents and give positive feedback, you will get results. You will inspire. You will ignite new ideas. And in return, your team wants to deliver more and grow.

Throughout her entrepreneurial journey, Amy Lisewski, the founder of Finest City Improv, has realized that she can't do it all alone. She places a strong focus on building and leading her team.

"We are only as strong as the team that we have assembled," said Amy. "So your job if you are building a company is to find the best people you can that have various strengths and various experiences, and ensure that they are rockstars."

Most importantly, you want to give honest feedback instead of simply being nice. I can't tell you how many of my student editors worry that they are being mean to their writers. As long as your feedback stems from a place of gratitude for the hard work and you take the time to identify what's working, you can remain honest—and that honesty will be appreciated.

ACTION:

Who are three leaders that inspire you? What qualities do you believe makes them successful leaders? Write it down!

Leaders are people too

As a leader, I focus on proactive communication and building meaningful relationships within our team. We are always working to better understand each other and where people are coming from. For example, before a writer even has the chance to miss a deadline, I'll encourage my editor to give that writer a call and find out more about them. What are they passionate about? What are their goals for their time at *College Magazine*? And if that writer *does* miss a deadline, the ensuing conversation will come from a greater place of understanding on both sides. I admired Blanchard's advice and I aim every day to lead by continuing to invest in my people.

In a leadership position, it's important to remember that you are leading *people* with complex lives and emotions. Spend the time getting to really know your team.

I can't tell you how many times an editor will say their writer has turned in a half-written draft without any source work or quotes. In other words, they're slacking. But the editor can't even tell me what the writer's major is, what clubs they are involved in, or even what that writer likes to do for fun.

For an editor in these shoes, I suggest setting up a meeting, asking meaningful questions, and getting to know the writer. When you spend that time to get to know your team, you build the foundation of a long-term relationship. When you understand what someone is passionate about, you can reframe their position to fit with their personal goals and interests. If there's a fit, they'll show up and put in the effort.

As a leader, you want to share about yourself. You're a person, too. And you're not perfect. I'm not saying you should air all your dirty laundry but try to show your human side too. You have family plans and weekend hobbies just like your team members. Share about a time that you made mistakes. Tell your team that when you get stressed out or have deadlines completely slip your mind, you have the tendency to shamelessly eat an entire sleeve of Girl Scout cookies. Let them see that you're a real person. When you build this relationship and share your authentic self, your team will feel more connected to you and your vision. They will show up for the hard work.

Even though the leader sets the vision, the leader must also be open to new ideas and feedback. I always ask for feedback and am open to hearing it. I let every member of our team know that they are shaping the direction of *College Magazine*—and I mean it. We let our students and team take on as much responsibility as they crave and can imagine.

Kevin Plank, founder of Under Armour, shared another tip with me when I met with him and the other past winners of the Cupid's Cup competition at his headquarters. He had us seated at a round table and said this was intentional; he didn't need a position at the head of the table for his team to know who was leading. He explained that he has created the sand box that is Under Armour, but he has ignited all of his team to build the castle that they dream of, no matter how high.

I've taken this advice and created that sandbox for everyone at *College Magazine*. Allow your team to take the initiative to grow their individual skills while also building upon the main vision.

I've had students suggest an entirely new vibe, article structure, training segment, video concept, and more. And I've let them take their ideas and run with them. These ideas have shaped *College Magazine* into what it is today, and it's the students who have pitched these ideas and taken these initiatives who are killing it in real world today. They are fearless.

ACTION:

How will you be a fearless leader? Write it down!

Congrats, yes you!

Congratulations on making the commitment to your qualified journey. I am highkey excited for you to take action today!

Remember the story I shared of taking a pay cut to start my business? The day I accidentally dropped a heavy box of magazines and got beat-up by a dolly? Or that time I was 0-3 on those internships? I'm glad you forgot, I certainly didn't. There have been numerous times where I've failed and wanted to give up on my intentional career journey. Facing rejection can eat away at your self-esteem, and I could write an entire book on that alone. Remember, it's not personal. You can learn from rejections by asking for feedback, but don't take it personally. The key is to push past the rejections and keep going, fueled by your passion. I kept going because I've unearthed my passion and declared my vision for my intentional career. I built my own qualified and if I can do it, you can too.

I don't think I've sugar coated this journey for you. But I did break it down to make it digestible. It's feasible, and anyone can follow these steps.

If you feel like you've followed every step in this book and you still can't imagine your future career, don't worry; I've got your back. My team and I have researched 100 organizations in top cities for just about every passion imaginable. If you find something that speaks to you, reach out and connect courageously.

Now that you've awakened the zombie, went BIG on your vision, and are making courageous connections every day, pass it on! Help someone else see just how qualified they are for what they want.

Think back to a time when someone reminded you, "you are good enough." Think about what that did for you. And now consider how you can inspire someone else to take action on their dreams. I know I needed to hear it and I think you do too.

Imagine a world where we all feel qualified to go after what we want. There's a ripple effect— when we love what we do, we make a greater impact in the world.

P.S.

WHEN THE WORLD IS SPIRALING

As I write these words, I'm living in the middle of a pandemic. One in four of Americans are unemployed. It's not safe to meet IRL. Life will throw you curveballs that may upend your plans. It may force you to start over, to double back, to reinvent your career journey.

Don't sweat it. If you've been using the tips I've shared throughout this entire book, you'll be A-OK. It might not happen overnight. But you'll know what to do and where to begin.

Even in a worldwide pandemic, you can still send a DM-a-day and make courageous connections. You can still build your personal branded website, renovate your resume, glow up your Insta, and launch your podcast. You can interview like a boss, even if it's on Zoom. And you can always build your qualified.

I promise that no matter what life throws at you, your qualified mindset is here to stay.

100 PASSION CAREER OPPORTUNITIES

To help you succeed, my team and I have uncovered 100 passion careers. This list will inspire your career search. We sought creative organizations with 100 or fewer employees that range in industry in top U.S. cities for recent graduates. This way you can see just how many opportunities exist that you didn't already know about.

Go to https://amandanachman.com/100 to download the full list.

ACKNOWLEDGEMENTS

The journey to writing Qualified all started when I was just a 22-year-old with a crazy idea to make a magazine. I'm eternally grateful to everyone who believed in 22-year-old me. Thank you to my friends, family and mentors who have been with me through the rollercoaster of entrepreneurship over the last thirteen years. Your support, encouragement and excitement for *College Magazine* and the message of Qualified has fueled me every step of the way.

To my publisher, Jesse Krieger, for your confidence in me and the first draft of Qualified. Thank you for your immense publishing industry wisdom and patience every step of the way. And to the team at Lifestyle Entrepreneurs Press, for your exceptional design and creative support.

To my publicist Laura Marie for making Qualified shine brighter than I could have ever imagined in my wildest dreams. Thank you for your shared love for Qualified and for always hyping me up with your words of encouragement. I am still pinching myself over Good Morning America.

To my editor Riley Bogh for falling madly in love with Qualified and injecting your humor and creativity at every moment possible. Thank you for taking the manuscript to the next level.

To my first read editors Rachel Aldrich and Taylor Ulrich, for taking a chance on this manuscript because you believed in my vision and for giving honest feedback. Your edits have been invaluable. Thank you both for your shared passion and support for all my many projects.

Thank you to Natalie DaRe, Josh Axelrod, Celina Pelaez Arias, Daniel Kuhn, Lauren Roberts, Natalie Janji, Macey Spensley, and Alexandra Blackwell for your edits and comments on my earliest drafts; I am proud to have met and worked with such gifted editors who share a similar passion for the written word and a commitment to quality writing.

I am so lucky to have found once-in-a-lifetime friends who make me smile even when life feels upside down. They remind me of my purpose, point out the wins along the way, and have challenged me with thoughtful feedback. They listened to my TEDx talk when the slides were still in serif font and even bought in to my quirky ideas like a chapter brainstorm party. They've seen just about every iteration of book cover design and believed in the project from the start. Thank you, Kari Gold, my best friend who has been there since our Blue Star Camp days. From hand distributing thousands of magazines, to cheering me on speaking at live virtual courses, to Zoom TEDx rehearsals—you are my person and your friendship means the world to me. To Abbey Liu, Margot Wohl, Morgan Miles, Sean Miles, Lillian Stuart, Belle Tekeli, Eddie Bosheh, Yaron Guez, Erica Ruhland, Conor Buttler-Ricketts for your coffee work dates, honest feedback, enthusiasm and ideas, but most of all, your friendship. Thank you to Hanhvy Bui, Jen Mino-Mirowitz, Ali Williams, Debra Schaffer,

Andrea Stone for your love and support. I am who I surround myself by and your level of laughter and kindness is a bar that I will forever be grateful to hold myself to as your friend.

To the Qualified PR and social media intern team, Anan Hussein, Kalyn Womack and Sydney Foster; thank you for your incredible hard work and dedication to the Qualified message.

To everyone at Influx in San Diego for providing a welcoming space and community where a majority of this book was written. To my fellow entrepreneurs who opened doors and shared knowledge including Per Larson, Lisa Abramson, and David Schmeltzle.

All editors and writers at *College Magazine* over the last thirteen years, if I haven't told you this enough—you are more qualified than you realize. Your journey has inspired me to write this book. I am so proud of your hard work and growth over the years; you continue to amaze me every day. Thank you for your continued dedication to changing the world through the written word. Making my vision reality took endless collaboration and millions of ideas from talented individuals—I couldn't have made it happen without you.

To Chris Testa for dedicating your senior year to *College Magazine* with me, drafting that first business plan together and your continued support. To Les Kollegian and the team at Jacob Tyler for believing in me and building the brand identity of *College Magazine* from the very start.

To anyone who has ever helped hand-distribute *College Magazine* with me including Kari Gold, Erin Cockren, and Rachel Wood. To my mom, Caren Nachman, for driving me around to hundreds of campus buildings in D.C. and Baltimore to drop off boxes upon boxes of magazines. You all know exactly how much love and sweat went into this project. Thank you.

To the University of Maryland and the Dingman Center for Entrepreneurship for your incredible support through the years. To Asher

Epstein for your confidence in *College Magazine* from that very first business plan pitch to today. Thank you for always being just a phone call away to reality check me and guide me in all my next power moves.

Thank you to each and every person who shared their story on my podcast or through interviews with me for this book.

To my teachers at Summit Park Elementary, Sudbrook Middle, Pikesville High, Carver Centre for Arts & Technology and the University of Maryland, I am so grateful for you. Thank you for sharing your gifts through your passion for education. Thank you for the immense impact you've had in my life by believing in me as your student. Special thank you to Christina Sundvall-Bartolomeo, Cecilia Terlizzi, and Professor Sandy Mack for encouraging my creativity and passion for the arts in all of its many forms.

To my parents who taught me to have big ideas and to follow my dreams. To my siblings Sherry, Jeff, Yan, and Jeffrey for always having my back. To Nathan, Emily, Avery and Ethan for being the sweetest and silliest nieces and nephews. I love you all so much.

To Austin and Frankie for your unconditional support, nose nudges, and warmth. You napped while I worked, reminding me of the importance of taking a break. You helped me appreciate the little things in life, like picnic blankets at the dog beach.

My deepest gratitude to you, my dear reader for giving these words your time. You are more qualified than you realize. I hope that by now you see it too. Come back any time you need a reminder.

Keep believing in yourself. Go after your dreams. You got this. Cheers!

References

1. Kross, E., Berman, M., Mischel, W., Smith, E., Wagner, T. (2011). Social Rejection Shares Somatosensory Representations with Physical Pain. *Proceedings of the National Academy of Sciences.*

2. Kubau, R., Sniezek, J., Zack, M. M., Lucas, R. E., & Burns, A. (2010). Well-Being Assessment: An Evaluation of Well-Being Scales for Public Health and Population Estimates of Well-Being among US Adults. *Applied Psychology: Health and Well-Being.*

3. Smith, E. E. (2013, January 9). There's More to Life Than Being Happy. *The Atlantic.* Retrieved from https://www.theatlantic.com/health/archive/2013/01/ theres-more-to-life-than-being-happy/266805/.

4. Kaufman, W. (2011, February 3). A Successful Job Search: It's All About Networking. *NPR.* Retrieved from https://www.npr. org/2011/02/08/133474431/a-successful-job-search-its-all-about-networking.

5. NAICS Association. (2019). *US Business Firmographics – Company Size.* Retrieved from https://www.naics.com/business-lists/ counts-by-company-size/.

6. Bureau of Labor Statistics, U. S. Department of Labor. (2017). *Number of Jobs, Labor Market Experience, and Earnings Growth Among Americans at 50: Results From a Longitudinal Survey.* [Press release]. Retrieved from https://www.bls.gov/news.release/pdf/ nlsoy.pdf.

7. Bureau of Labor Statistics, United States Department of Labor. (2018). *Employee Tenure in 2018.* [Press release]. Retrieved from https://www.bls.gov/news.release/tenure.nr0.htm.

8. Marks & Spencer. (2017). *Research Reveals 96% of The UK is Living Life on Autopilot as M&S Launches 'Make It Matter Day' on 1 June 2017*. [Press release]. Retrieved from https://corporate.marksandspencer.com/media/press-releases/2017/make-it-matter-day.

9. Strada-Gallup 2017 College Student Survey. (n.d.). Retrieved from https://news.gallup.com/reports/225161/2017-strada-gallup-college-student-survey.aspx.

10. NCAA Recruiting Facts. (2018). [Graphic summary of Division I, II, III college sports and quick facts about the universities]. Retrieved from https://www.ncaa.org/sites/default/files/Recruiting%20Fact%20Sheet%20WEB.pdf.

11. Ignatova, M. (2019, March 5). New Report: Women Apply to Fewer Jobs Than Men, But Are More Likely to Get Hired. Retrieved from https:// business.linkedin.com/talent-solutions/blog/diversity/2019/how-women-find-jobs-gender-report.

12. Gamedesigning. (2019). Retrieved from https://www.gamedesigning.org/.

13. Study.com. (2020, January 20). *Most Competitive Careers.* Retrieved from https://study.com/articles/most_competitive_careers.html.

14. Miller, S. (2013). Navigating the Business of Dance. *Backstage.* Retrieved from https://www.backstage.com/magazine/article/navigating-business-dance-15253/.

15. United States Department of Labor, Bureau of Labor Statistics. (2019). *Fastest Growing Occupations*. Retrieved from https://www.bls.gov/ooh/fastest-growing.htm.

16. Wikipedia contributors. (2019, April 28). Human Rights Campaign. In *Wikipedia, The Free Encyclopedia*. Retrieved 3:27, May 2, 2019, from https://en.wikipedia.org/wiki/Human_Rights_Campaign.

17. Vozza, S. (2014, February 25). Personal Mission Statements of 5 Famous CEOs (And Why You Should Write One Too). *Fast Company*. Retrieved from https://www.fastcompany.com/3026791/personal-mission-statements-of-5-famous-ceos-and-why-you-should-write-one-too.

18. Suttie, J. (2015, December 7). How Smartphones Are Killing Conversation: A Q&A with MIT professor Sherry Turkle about her new book, *Reclaiming Conversation. Greater Good Magazine*. Retrieved from https://greatergood.berkeley.edu/article/item/how_smartphones_are_killing_conversation.

19. The Adler Group Articles. (n.d.). New Survey Reveals 85% of All Jobs are Filled Via Networking. Retrieved from https://louadlergroup.com/new-survey-reveals-85-of-all-jobs-are-filled-via-networking/.

20. Ward, A. F. (2013, July 16). The Neuroscience of Everybody's Favorite Topic. *Scientific American*. Retrieved from https://www.scientificamerican.com/article/the-neuroscience-of-everybody-favorite-topic-themselves/.

21. Huang, K., Yeomans, M., Brooks, A.W., Minson, J., & Gino, F. (2017). It Doesn't Hurt to Ask: Question-asking Increases Liking [Abstract]. *Journal of Personality and Social Psychology 113* (3): 430-452.

22. Peters, T. (1997, August 31). The Brand Called You. *Fast Company*. Retrieved from https://www.fastcompany.com/28905/brand-called-you.

23. Heater, B. (2018, June 5). Apple Podcasts now

hosts more than 550,000 active shows. *Tech Crunch*. Retrieved from https://techcrunch.com/2018/06/05/apple-podcasts-now-hosts-more-than-555000-active-shows/.

24. Peiser, J. (2019, March 6). Podcast Growth is Popping in the U.S., Survey Shows. *The New York Times*. Retrieved from https://www.nytimes.com/2019/03/06/business/media/podcast-growth.html.

25. The Deloitte Millennial Survey 2017. *Deloitte*. Retrieved from https://www2.deloitte.com/il/en/pages/about-deloitte/articles/millennialsurvey.html.

CPSIA information can be obtained
at www.ICGtesting.com
Printed in the USA
JSHW032305040820
7112JS00003B/24